Brandeis at 150

Brandeis in 1914. *Harris and Ewing photograph, Collection of the Supreme Court of the United States.*

BRANDEIS *at 150*

THE LOUISVILLE PERSPECTIVE

A SESQUICENTENNIAL COMMEMORATION

The Louis D. Brandeis School of Law

The University of Louisville

BUTLER BOOKS

ISBN 1-884532-76-4

Printed in Canada by Friesens Printers through Four Colour
Imports, Louisville, KY

For additional copies contact:
Butler Books
P.O. Box 7311
Louisville, KY 40207
502-897-9393

www.butlerbooks.com

Acknowledgments

In preparing this publication and the program, many individuals contributed in a number of ways.

Beginning in summer of 2004, a committee began planning for this occasion. The committee of Les Abramson, Joseph Ardery, Peter Scott Campbell, Joe Rooks Rapport, Laura Rothstein (Chair), Keith Runyon, and Kurt Metzmeier determined that having a daylong conference focusing on Justice Brandeis along with this publication were to be the key products of their planning. The purpose was not to showcase all of Justice Brandeis's numerous contributions, but rather to focus on some of the major issues for which he is known and some of the most interesting aspects of his life and to highlight his connection to Louisville.

In addition to the Underwriters and Supporters listed on page 8, the efforts of many others made this publication and program possible.

Dean David Ensign supported the Sesquicentennial program and the publication of the book, and contributed to the book through his essay on the "Art of Brandeis."

Historical information was drawn from previous law school histories prepared by Dean Donald Burnett, Dean Barbara Lewis and Professor Linda Ewald. Information from Tom Owen and others in the University of Louisville Archives was valuable in preparing this publication.

Information about the program was shared by the American Civil Liberties Union (Kentucky Chapter), the Filson Historical Society, the Supreme Court Historical Society, The Temple and the Louisville Bar Association.

Several individuals within the University of Louisville Communications Department and the Brandeis School of Law were particularly helpful in gathering photographs and other information for the publication. These include Laurel Harper, Tom Fougerousse, Cindy Vermillion, Bob Micou, Kristen Cundiff, Simone Beach and Becky Wimberg.

Table of Contents

Underwriters and Supporters

The following underwriters and supporters made this publication and program possible:

Mr. and Mrs. Owsley Brown

Creighton Mershon

Middleton Reutlinger

Rabbis Gaylia R. Rooks and Joe Rooks Rapport

Speaker funding provided by

Wilson W. and Anne D. Wyatt Distinguished Speakers Endowment

Lucille Little Endowment

Preface

Louis D. Brandeis was born on November 13, 1856, in Louisville, Kentucky. His earliest memories are of his mother serving food to Union soldiers in his front yard. He left Louisville at age 16 and later graduated from Harvard Law School, had a brilliant career as a practicing lawyer and advocate on behalf of numerous public causes, and became an Associate Justice of the Supreme Court in 1916, at age 60. He resigned from the Court in 1939, and died in 1941. He chose the law school as his final resting place.

Although he never returned to live in Louisville, family members and their descendants remained in Louisville, and he continued to be connected to his family, to Louisville, to the University of Louisville, and to the Law School. The Law School was renamed the Louis D. Brandeis School of Law in 1997.

With one of the most remarkable records of accomplishment of any American, Justice Brandeis is known for his attention to an enormous number of important issues. November 13, 2006, marks the 150th anniversary of his birth. It is an appropriate time to reflect on the noteworthy accomplishments of this remarkable native of Louisville and to recognize his connection and contributions to the world, the nation, Louisville, the University, and the School of Law.

Justice Stanley Reed, who grew up in Kentucky, laying the cornerstone for the Brandeis law school's main building on June 6, 1938. *Image © University of Kentucky, all rights reserved. Stanley Forman Reed Papers, 1926–1977, 81M3, Audio-Visual Archives, Special Collections and Digital Programs, University of Kentucky Libraries.*

The Brandeis Vision

and the University of Louisville

As the cornerstone for the law school building was laid in 1938, Dean Robert M. Miller noted, "It is hard for one who has not lived through the struggle of the law school to appreciate Mr. Justice Brandeis' influence and assistance. He always kept in the background, seeking no word of appreciation for himself or what he had done…his vision of the law school was as an active force in the community, rather than just another school turning out lawyers."

—From Oscar Bryant, *A Community at its Best*, UofL Magazine, p. 12 Spring 1997

The Brandeis Vision

Donald L. Burnett, Jr.
Dean 1990-2000
Louis D. Brandeis School of Law
University of Louisville

Reprinted with permission from Volume 37 Brandeis Law Journal Pages 1-7 (1998-1999)
Copyright © 1998 University of Louisville; Dean Donald L. Burnett, Jr.

He gave his books, his papers, his money, his time, and, ultimately, his last remains to a law school in the community where he was born. He had a vision for legal education. Today, in Louisville, the law school believed to be America's fifth oldest in continuous operation is graced by his name, and a law review now is ennobled by his legacy.

Louis Dembitz Brandeis was born in Louisville on November 13, 1856, a son of German immigrants. After graduating from Louisville's Male High School and studying three terms at the Annen-Realschule in Dresden, Germany, he was drawn to the study of law by his uncle, Lewis Dembitz—a noted practitioner, public citizen, and scholar who eventually published the landmark treatise, Kentucky Jurisprudence, in 1890. Young Brandeis enrolled at Harvard Law School, where he blossomed in the intellectually charged atmosphere of case analysis and Socratic dialogue created by Professor Christopher Columbus Langdell. "Law seems so interesting to me in all its aspects," Brandeis wrote to his sister Amy, "it is difficult for me to understand that any of the initiated should not burn with enthusiasm."[1] Following graduation with the highest honors, he worked briefly at a St. Louis law firm, then returned to Boston where he established his famous partnership with Samuel Warren; together, they combined the practice of law with a love of developing the law, as evidenced by their landmark article, "The Right to Privacy."[2]

Brandeis's career as a practitioner extended to 1916, when at the age of nearly sixty years—a time when some might think of concluding their life's work rather than opening a new chapter—he was appointed to the Supreme Court. There he served until 1939, expounding as a jurist on two interconnected themes he had developed as a lawyer: accepting responsibility and preserving liberty. He expressed his own sense of professional responsibility by resolving to devote the equivalent of at least one hour per day to public service, and he urged members of the bar to demonstrate "moral courage in the face of financial loss and personal ill-will to stand for right and justice."[3] This was no hollow preachment. He compensated his firm for his pro bono time, and his advocacy of social justice nearly deprived him later of the Senate's confirmation of his nomination to the Supreme Court.[4] (Once on the Court, however, his sense of judicial restraint occasionally caused him dutifully to uphold legislation that he disfavored.[5]) He also championed liberty, proclaiming individuals could grow to their full potential only when nurtured by freedom:

Those who won our independence believed that the final end of the State was to make men free to develop their faculties; and that in its government the deliberative forces should prevail over the arbitrary. They valued liberty both as an end and as a means. They believed liberty to be the secret of happiness and courage to be the secret of liberty.[6]

Upon these themes of responsibility and liberty, Brandeis constructed his well-known arguments against the abusive power of large financial trusts[7] and against the stultifying effects of large organizations upon human creativity.[8] He also built upon these themes to develop his concept of the lawyer as a public citizen. Reflecting a Jeffersonian view of democracy at a community scale, and echoing of de Tocqueville's praise of lawyers as the connectors of disparate elements in American communities, Brandeis charged the practicing bar to help society balance the assertion of individual rights with the assumption of collective responsibilities: "[I]t lies with our lawyers to say in what lines [progressive social] action shall be expressed: wisely and temperately or wildly and intemperately; in lines of evolution or in lines of revolution."[9] Here, in this dynamic challenge, was the source of enthusiasm Brandeis had felt in law school. Young people drawn to the legal profession, he later said, "may rest assured that they will find in it an opportunity for usefulness which is probably unequalled elsewhere. There is and there will be a call upon the legal profession to do a great work for this country."[10]

Preparing lawyers to do this "great work" occupied much of Justice

Brandeis's letters were unloaded at the law school on November 13, 1939.

Brandeis's concern. At a personal level, he became a treasured mentor to his law clerks, whose names eventually filled a pantheon of leaders in the bar, the academy, the business community, and public office.[11] Dean Acheson, a law clerk destined to become Secretary of State, later recalled the Justice speaking of his clerks "with all the tenderness of a father speaking of his sons. He entered so deeply into our lives because he took us so deeply into his."[12] More broadly, Justice Brandeis was interested in improving the institutions of legal education; indeed, his younger colleague, Felix Frankfurter, described him as "one of the few thinkers in the profession concerned with the fundamental problem of legal education."[13]

This photograph, taken around 1876, is probably Louis Brandeis as a law student at Harvard.

When Harvard law dean Roscoe Pound proposed to increase enrollments at that school, Justice Brandeis objected, calling instead for smaller, better schools.[14] As noted by biographer Philippa Strum, Brandeis responded "he wanted 'not a bigger H.L.S., but 20 Harvard Law Schools.' And he immediately set about creating one other Harvard, this one in Kentucky."[15]

In 1925, having already begun a series of gifts to the University of Louisville, Justice Brandeis wrote the time had come to "build a law school of distinction."[16] Founded in 1846, Louisville's law school already was in its eighth decade when Justice Brandeis began to invest in it. He gave the school his personal library, including many rare texts on early civil and common law; his personal papers, comprising approximately 250,000 items; and his money (even buying light fixtures when the law school was located in a downtown building, before moving to its current location on the Belknap campus in 1938). He also helped raise money from other donors; aided the school in obtaining the papers of Justice John Marshall Harlan, the "great dissenter;" arranged for the school to receive original briefs filed with the United States Supreme Court, a practice the Court still honors; and bequeathed a substantial part of his estate to the University of Louisville. After his death in 1941, his last remains—and later the remains of his wife, Alice Goldmark Brandeis—were buried unobtrusively beneath the law school's classical portico.[17]

To Justice Brandeis, the University of Louisville presented an opportunity to translate his fundamental beliefs about law and policy into a new vision for legal education. His distrust of "bigness," which had led him to reject Harvard Law School's expansion, moved him to envision at Louisville a more intimate learning environment where the law school could "devote itself to teaching the law in a fine and helpful way."[18] Similarly, his belief that creativity flourished outside large organizations led him to predict that the states, rather than the national government, would become the principal incubators of new ideas in public policy.[19] He urged universities and law schools to support this grass-roots creativity. One of Justice Brandeis's close collaborators in Louisville, Robert N. Miller, explained the Justice's concept of this role for legal education generally and for the University of Louisville's law school in particular:

> [A law school should] be one of the leaders of legal thought in the state . . . an influence tending to maintain the highest standards of legal and judicial thought and policy; among other services it can render, it will be ready with wise advice with regard to the new legislation which changing conditions from time to time may require. . . . Such a school may be at the same time closely in touch with modern thought everywhere, and yet an integral part of Kentucky, Kentuckian to the backbone. A law school which rises to the point of fully meeting the needs of its own state will find itself honored by the respectful admiration of all other states. In solving its home problems with distinction, it acquires specialized knowledge of which even the proudest institutions of other states are glad to avail themselves. . . . .
> . . . Kentucky is a state where such an aim is not too ambitious to be realized.[20]

Drawing upon his experience as a practitioner and recognizing law is shaped significantly by societal forces, Justice Brandeis believed a lawyer's education must extend beyond the discipline of law itself:

> Knowledge of the decided cases and of the rules of logic cannot alone make a great lawyer. He must know, must feel "in his bones" the facts to which they apply must know, too, that if they do not stand the test of such application the logical result will somehow or other be avoided . . . .[21]

As a lawyer, Brandeis had pioneered this interdisciplinary approach with his "Brandeis Briefs," which wove legal arguments together with empirical evidence and with insights drawn from the disciplines of economics and sociology.[22] To Brandeis, this crossing of disciplinary boundaries was not an intellectual affectation; it was a fulfillment of the lawyer's duty to master the facts.[23]

Finally, as one of America's most widely recognized lawyers engaging in service pro bono publico, Brandeis believed that law schools should cultivate an appreciation of service as a professional obligation. In his famous address, "The Opportunity in the Law," delivered to the Harvard Ethical Society in 1905, he argued that "whole training" in law school should include not only the development of reason and judgment, but also the inculcation of a commitment to the legal profession's public trust.[24] He lamented that many lawyers had neglected this trust, representing the nation's moneyed interests "while the public is often inadequately represented or wholly unrepresented."[25] Those words remain timely;

today, the law school named for Justice Brandeis features one of the country's first five mandatory public service programs.

The University of Louisville is not yet finished responding to Justice Brandeis's ambitious agenda. As noted by the law faculty in their resolution embracing the Brandeis name, "[t]he legacy of Justice Brandeis has been an historic foundation of the School of Law and is an inspiring charter for its future."[26] To the elements of the Brandeis vision—collegial teaching and learning, policy development, interdisciplinary study, and an ethic of public service—it is now appropriate to add a distinguished law review bearing his name. Justice Brandeis evinced a special understanding of the importance of law reviews when, in 1917, he became the first member of the Supreme Court to cite law review articles in a judicial opinion.[27] He regarded law reviews, not only as avenues of discourse among scholars, but also as bridges connecting the academy with the legal profession, the judiciary, and the venues of public policy.

Building upon the scholarly foundation of its predecessor, the University of Louisville's Journal of Family Law, the new Brandeis Law Journal will serve all the purposes of a multi-subject, "mainstream" law review. It also will provide a uniquely appropriate forum for examining topics such as ethics in public service, problems in social justice, development of public policy, issues in federalism, and interdisciplinary perspectives on law and the performance of legal institutions that resonate with the Brandeis legacy. In all of its dimensions the Brandeis Law Journal, like the towering figure for whom it is named, will search for truth, pursue justice, and encourage minds to be bold. If it can be said that any legal publication has a spirit, then let the spirit of this Journal soar as high as Justice Brandeis's hopes for our school and our profession:

> To realize the promise of America through law that [all] might share to the limit of their capacity in the American adventure was the end to which he devoted all his talents and his energies. In him the lawyer's genius was dedicated to the prophet's vision, and the fusion produced a magnificent weapon for righteousness. In his hand the sword was fringed with fire.[28]

1. Letter from Louis D. Brandeis to Amy Brandeis Wehle (Jan. 20, 1877), in 1 Letters of Louis D. Brandeis 14 (Melvin I. Urofsky & David W. Levy eds., 1971-1978).
2. Louis D. Brandeis & Samuel D. Warren, The Right to Privacy, 4 Harv. L. Rev. 193 (1890).
3. Melvin I. Urofsky, Louis D. Brandeis and the Progressive Tradition 16 (1981).
4. See Bruce Allen Murphy, The Brandeis/Frankfurter Connection: The Secret Political Activities of Two Supreme Court Justices 22 (1982); Lewis J. Paper, Brandeis 209-40 (1983).
5. See Paul A. Freund, Mr. Justice Brandeis: A Centennial Memoir, 70 Harv. L. Rev. 769, 786-87 (1957).
6. Whitney v. California, 274 U.S. 357, 375 (1927) (Brandeis, J., concurring).
7. See Louis D. Brandeis, Other People's Money (1914).
8. See The Curse of Bigness: Miscellaneous Papers of Louis D. Brandeis (Osmond K. Fraenkel ed., 1934).
9. Bernard Flexner, Mr. Justice Brandeis and the University of Louisville 65 (1938) (quoting Ernest Poole, Brandeis, Am. Mag., Feb. 1911).
10. Id.
11. See Gene Teitelbaum, Justice Louis D. Brandeis: A Bibliography of Writings and Other Materials on the Justice 125 (1988), for an illuminating list of the Brandeis clerks.
12. Dean Acheson, Mr. Justice Brandeis, 55 Harv. L. Rev. 191, 191 (1941) (Address delivered at the funeral services, Oct.7, 1941).
13. Nelson Lloyd Dawson, Louis D. Brandeis, Felix Frankfurter and the New Deal 3-4 (1980).
14. See Philippa Strum, Louis D. Brandeis: Justice for the People 398 (1984) [hereinafter Strum, Justice for the People].
15. Id.
16. Flexner, supra note 9, at 70.
17. See Barbara B. Lewis et al., School of Law Sesquicentennial History and Law Alumni/ae Directory at xvii-xxi (1996).
18. Flexner, supra note 9, at 71.
19. Thus, in his memorable dissenting opinion in New State Ice Co. v. Liebmann, 285 U.S. 262 (1932), Justice Brandeis observed:

    It is one of the happy incidents of the federal system that a single courageous state may, if its citizens choose, serve as a laboratory; and try novel social and economic experiments without risk to the rest of the country. This Court has the power to prevent an experiment. . . . But, in the exercise of this high power, we must be ever on our guard, lest we erect our prejudices into legal principles. If we would guide by the light of reason, we must let our minds be bold. Id. At 311.
20. Flexner, supra note 9, at 61-62.
21. Urofsky, supra note 3, at 7.
22. See Philippa Strum, Brandeis and the Living Constitution, in Brandeis and America 120 (Nelson L. Dawson ed., 1989).
23. See id.
24. See Strum, Justice for the People, supra note 14, at 40-41.
25. See id.
26. Resolution of the Law Faculty, University of Louisville, Feb. 24, 1997.
27. See Adams v. Tanner, 244 U.S. 590, 597, 603, 613 nn.1-3, 615 n.1 (1917) (Brandeis, J., dissenting).
28. Paul A. Freund, Memorial Tributes to Mr. Justice Brandeis, Proceedings of the Bar of the Supreme Court of the United States, in The Brandeis Reader 234 (Ervin H. Pollack ed., 1956).

LOUIS D. BRANDEIS SCHOOL OF LAW

UNIVERSITY of LOUISVILLE

BRANDEIS

LAW JOURNAL

VOLUME 42 – NUMBER 4 • SUMMER ISSUE 2004

The Brandeis Law Journal, built on the scholarly foundation of its predecessor, the Journal of Family Law, published its inaugural volume in 1998.

"*Growth* cannot be imposed upon the University. It must proceed from within. The desire for worthy growth must be deeply felt by the executive officers and members of the faculty. It must be they who raise the University standards and extend its influence. But the desire may be stimulated by suggestion and the achievement may be furthered by friendly aid."

—*Letter to Alfred Brandeis, February 18, 1925*

"A Good Name is Rather to Be Chosen Than Great Riches":
The Louis D. Brandeis School of Law at the University of Louisville

Melvin I. Urofsky
Professor of History and Public Policy
Virginia Commonwealth University and
Adjunct Professor of Law
University of Richmond Law School

Were Louis Brandeis to return to life he would, I think, be appalled at much of what the United States has become. The man who spoke out so forcefully against the "curse of bigness"[1] would find an America where bigness is the dominant characteristic—big government, big business, big cities, and big shopping malls, to name just a few. The archfoe of monopoly[2] would not find anything to cheer about in the mania merger that has swept over the United States in the last few years. The reformer who paid his own law firm for the time he devoted to public service[3] would weep at the current moral position of government leaders at every level. And the man who took pride in the fact that the Supreme Court was the only government body where each judge did his own work, aided by a single clerk,[4] would no doubt weep at what Justice Lewis Powell once described as the nine law offices occupying the Marble Palace[5] (a building, by the way, which Brandeis not only opposed erecting, but then refused to occupy).

But I do feel the Justice would be pleased by the University of Louisville and its law school. Despite his well-known penchant for denying requests to name buildings, professorships, and other edifices after him,[6] I think he would take a quiet satisfaction in the renaming of the University of Louisville School of Law to the Louis D. Brandeis Law School. His dream for the University, which he spelled out in a series of memoranda to family members and others,[7] was for a regional school that would provide excellence in its instruction and instill in its students a sense of service to the community. These goals were valid when Brandeis first articulated them nearly three-quarters of a century ago, and they are still valid today.

On this occasion it is worth pausing for a moment to recall Louis Brandeis's ideals about the law and his great expectations for law schools. These are the benchmarks against which the law school that now bears his name should be judged.

From the time he entered the Harvard Law School in September 1875, Brandeis was enamored with the law. He wrote long letters to his family extolling the law school, as well as the law. To his brother-in-law Otto A. Wehle, also an attorney, Brandeis wrote, "how well I am pleased with everything that pertains to the law .... My thoughts are almost entirely occupied by the law . . . ."[8] As for Harvard, he thought the law school provided the great opportunity "to associate with young men who have the same interest and ambition, who are determined to make as great progress as possible in their studies and devote all their time to the same."[9] At a time when many young men prepared for the bar by "reading" in the offices of established lawyers, Brandeis confidently declared that "I doubt not, that one can learn very much in an office—That first year at law is, however, surely ill-spent in an office."[10] It was a view he held throughout his life, and when his daughter Susan asked him whether she should take time off from law school to work in an office, he forcefully vetoed the idea.[11]

Once in practice, Brandeis enjoyed great success at the bar. He was one of the top six moneymakers among Boston lawyers, and, in 1890, at the age of thirty-four, he earned more than $50,000 a year, at a time when three-fourths of the lawyers in the country made less than $5,000 annually.[12] Brandeis never looked down his nose at material success; he had no use, however, for those who saw the law as nothing more than a means of making money.

What made Brandeis different is that he looked beyond the confines of legal practice to the greater society. He believed strongly that the law and life could not be artificially separated. In an age of increasingly narrow specialization, he remained a generalist. Moreover, he felt obligated not only to be counsel to his clients, but to serve the public as well.[13]

Oliver Wendell Holmes, Jr., in his famous Lowell Lecture, had sounded the clarion for what came to be called sociological jurisprudence, the effort to relate legal doctrine and change to the larger changes going on in society.[14] While reformers and academics thrilled at Holmes's statement that "the felt necessities of the time" drove legal theory, most lawyers clung to a formalistic theory of an unchanging law governed only by an unfettered market. When Brandeis wanted to present his ideas to the annual meetings of the American Bar Association on the responsibilities of lawyers to the public, the officers politely but firmly turned him down.[15] So Brandeis spoke at the Harvard Ethical Society and attacked the dominant practice of the American bar:

> Instead of holding a position of independence, between the wealthy and the people, prepared to curb the excesses of either, able lawyers have, to a large extent, allowed themselves to become adjuncts of great corporations and have neglected their obligation to use their powers for the protection of the people. We hear much of the "corporation lawyer," and far too little of the "people's lawyer." The great opportunity of the American bar is and will be to stand again as it did in the past, ready to protect also the interests of the people.
>
> . . . .
>
> . . . The leading lawyers of the United States have been engaged mainly in supporting the claims of the corporations; often in endeavoring to evade or nullify the extremely crude laws by which legislators sought to regulate the power or curb the excesses of corporations . . . .[16]

Brandeis did not just preach these words; he lived them, and in the two decades before he went onto the bench he justly earned the title of "the people's lawyer."[17] It was in that guise that he pioneered the "Brandeis brief," using social and economic data to justify the legislatures' efforts to meliorate the worst aspects of industrialization.[18] He struck many people as strange when he refused to accept fees for his public work, but we can trace the real beginning of pro bono work in this country from his efforts in the years before World War One.[19]

There is one other aspect—out of many—about Brandeis's philosophy of law that is worth mentioning here—his insistence on the moral soundness of his position. The law profession today is not held in high regard by the public, and lawyers are often described as "sharks" or "barracudas," hired guns working for whomever will pay them a high fee. Our adversarial system of justice assumes, even demands, that both sides coming before a court have legal backing, and therefore some rightness in their claims. The purpose of lawyers is to present their client's case and persuade either judge or jury that their legal argument is better, or more just, than that of their opponents. As the profession became more specialized in the latter nineteenth century, lawyers ceased to act as counsel and acted as the mere technicians they had become, evading moral questions by the assumption that some right must exist on both sides.

Brandeis, both in his public and private work, would act only when he believed in the legitimacy of his clients' cases. When people came to him who were clearly in the wrong, he would tell them so, and try to get them to see that their best interests in the long run would be to do the right thing. When one of his clients went bankrupt, Brandeis agreed to assist the family only after they had pledged they wanted the fairest settlement possible for their creditors.[20] Even the then-normal practices of the bar were not sacred when he believed them wrong, and, as a young attorney, he angered many of his colleagues by attacking a cost-reimbursement feature of one case.[21] As my colleague and co-editor David Levy points out, Brandeis, by his example, asked lawyers to start making moral judgments and to stop turning their backs on complex situations.[22] In a 1907 address, he declared: "What the lawyer needs to redeem himself is not more ability or physical courage but the moral courage in the face of financial loss and personal ill-will to stand for right and justice."[23]

And where would lawyers learn these habits? Brandeis hoped they would be exposed to high moral and ethical standards in the law schools along with high quality instruction. I am afraid that he would be rather disappointed today at the near minimal exposure students get to professional ethics. In many law schools it is a required course, but worth only one credit, and often taught by adjunct instructors. Brandeis certainly hoped that the University of Louisville and its law school would meet the high standards he had set for himself and which he hoped would one day permeate the entire profession.

Through his letters, we can trace Brandeis's involvement in the growth of the University of Louisville, and his goals for its various components, especially the law school. On September 24, 1924, Brandeis wrote to his niece, Adele, that he had shipped three large cases of books and documents to the University, and that more would be shipped soon.

This letter to his brother Alfred is the letter that best describes his plans for UofL. It includes the line, "Money alone cannot buy a worthy university…" The full text of the letter can be found on page 163 of volume V of The Letters of Louis D. Brandeis, 5 volumes, *edited by Melvin I. Urofsky and David W. Levy.*

Since there was no card file available, he was enclosing a check for one thousand dollars to defray the expenses of preparing an adequate catalogue, necessary rebinding, and for related clerical and other expenses. Many of these materials were government reports, which Brandeis had been collecting for many years.[24] Thus overnight, the University of Louisville acquired an important library collection, well before the government began designating official repositories for government documents.

With this step Brandeis undertook to help the University, a project to which he devoted himself throughout the 1920s. He brought to the enterprise the same energy and enthusiasm, and, above all, attention to detail that he had earlier brought to his various social and economic reforms. Because of distance, as well as the limits on direct action imposed by judicial propriety, he operated through intermediaries, especially his brother Alfred's family, and after Alfred's death in 1928, primarily through Fannie Brandeis, one of Alfred's four daughters.

Brandeis never believed in, to use a phrase from a later period, "throwing money" at a problem. He understood that while universities, especially new universities, needed money, other ways existed in which benefactors could help build a strong and enduring institution. He donated what would be the cores of several specialized collections, and, through Alfred, secured donations of similar core collections in various fields. Without a good library, the University would never be able to attract superior faculty and students—the two ingredients Brandeis considered essential in a great school.

The most complete statement of Brandeis's philosophy is found in a letter to his brother on February 18, 1925, in which he wrote the following:

> Money alone cannot build a worthy university. Too much money, or too quick money, may mar one; particularly if it is foreign money. To become great, a university must express the people whom it serves, and must express the people and the community at their best. The aim must be high and the vision broad; the goal seemingly attainable but beyond the immediate reach. It was with these requisites in mind that I made the three essays referred to . . . . History teaches, I believe, that the present tendency toward centralization must be arrested, if we are to attain the American ideals, and that for it must be substituted intense development of life through activities in the several states and localities. The problem is a very difficult one; but the local university is the most hopeful instrument for any attempt at solution.
>
> Our university can become great, and serve this end, only if it is essentially Kentuckian-an institution for Kentuckians, developed by Kentuckians. For this reason, everything in the life of the State is worthy of special enquiry. Every noble memory must be cherished . . . .
>
> Growth cannot be imposed upon the University. It must proceed mainly from within. The desire for worthy growth must be deeply felt by the executive officers and members of the faculty. It must be they who raise the University to standards and extend its usefulness . . . .[25]

At the same time that Brandeis worked with his family to develop the University of Louisville, he became involved in an important policy debate at his alma mater, the Harvard Law School. What he said and did there is instructive in appreciating his dreams for Louisville.

In April 1922, Felix Frankfurter wrote to Brandeis about funds for the Law School. Brandeis wrote back that he would be "glad to contribute to any or all of the small Law School funds," since he considered them a distinct asset of the School "which may be made to serve an important purpose," namely, "to bind successful graduates and others to the School, by keeping them alive to its growth and problems."[26] He emphasized that, at least for the present, "it would be undesirable to have the needs met either (a) from income of a general endowment, or (b) from gifts of the whole amount from single individuals, or (c) from funds derived through increasing tuition fees."[27] The "recurrent need must be preserved," he told Frankfurter, so that the School should have to call on its graduates each year, and this, in turn, would bind the graduates ever closer to the School.[28] Today, of course, any development officer would gasp at this idea. No writing of 10,000 checks for $100 apiece; just write one check for $1,000,000. But Brandeis did not see law schools as objects of philanthropy, although he recognized that some demands, such as new buildings, could and should be met by large gifts. Rather, he viewed law schools as organic entities bonding with students, not just during two or three years of classes, but throughout their lives. Law schools should be part of the communal life, and the sons and daughters of those schools needed constant reminders of how much they were needed.

Thus, when Dean Roscoe Pound decided that Harvard's reputation as a national law school could only be sustained by making the law school bigger, admitting more students, and hiring more faculty,[29] Brandeis was aghast. He urged Felix Frankfurter and others to oppose the plan and wrote that one must make "frank recognition of the fact that the numbers in excess of 1000, and the proposed 350 seat lecture halls & lectures, are irreconcilable with H[arvard] L[aw] S[chool]'s traditions & aims."[30] He also lobbied his colleagues, such as Justice Edward T. Sanford, who had graduated from Harvard in 1889, to oppose the expansion plans.[31] Brandeis did not want one huge Harvard Law School, but many small schools emulating Harvard's excellence.

It would not be fair to say that Brandeis wanted nothing more from the law school at Louisville than that it be a "little-Harvard-on-the-Ohio."[32] As should be clear from his letters to his family, the University of Louisville should be the intellectual beacon for the community, and to do so it had to adapt to and meet local needs. The qualities he believed worth emulating from Harvard were ones of quality in instruction and resources, but just as Harvard had been supported by Boston for nearly three hundred years, so the University of Louisville could achieve greatness if it tied its future to those of the people it served. The Bible tells us "a good name is rather to be chosen than great riches,"[33] and the University of Louisville's law school has chosen a good name. Brandeis wanted the institution that now bears his name to teach its students the glory of the law and its possibilities for achieving social justice. He wanted it to train attorneys who could go out and do well for themselves financially, but more importantly to do good for the community. Those are the standards by which the Louis D. Brandeis School of Law at the University of Louisville must judge its success.

1. See The Curse of Bigness: Miscellaneous Writings of Louis D. Brandeis (Osmond K. Fraenkel ed., 1934).

2. See Louis D. Brandeis, Trusts, Efficiency, and the New Party, Colliers Nat'l Wkly., Sept. 14, 1912, at 14.

3. See Letter from Louis D. Brandeis to E. Louise Malloch (Nov. 4, 1907), in 2 Letters of Louis D. Brandeis 44 (Melvin I. Urofsky & David W. Levy eds., 1971-1978) [hereinafter Brandeis Letters].

4. See Letter from Louis D. Brandeis to Felix Frankfurter (Feb. 6, 1925), in Half Brother, Half Son: The Letters of Louis D. Brandeis to Felix Frankfurter 191 (Melvin I. Urofsky & David W. Levy eds., 1991) [hereinafter Half Brother].

5. Interview with Lewis F. Powell, Jr., United States Supreme Court Justice, in Charlottesville, Va. (Apr. 5, 1988).

6. See Alpheus Thomas Mason, Brandeis: A Free Man's Life 613-14 (1946). Brandeis consistently refused to accept honorary degrees, and Thurman Arnold told the following story:

> When I was on the faculty of the Yale law school they asked us to nominate a candidate for an honorary degree. The faculty named Justice Brandeis. President Angell turned it down. Next year they asked the faculty again. We named Justice Brandeis. President Angell gave in, but the trustees turned it down. The third year they asked us again. We named Justice Brandeis. President Angell approved, the trustees approved, but the corporation turned it down. The fourth year they asked us again. Again we named Justice Brandeis. President Angell approved, the trustees approved, the corporation approved, but Justice Brandeis turned it down . . . . When Harvard was arranging to have his portrait installed in the Law School alongside those of Marshall, Webster, and Holmes, Brandeis refused to sit. The artist had to work from a photograph . . . . Id.

7. The memoranda can be found beginning with a letter from Brandeis to Adele Brandeis on September 24, 1924. See Letter from Louis D. Brandeis to Adele Brandeis (Sept. 24, 1924), in 5 Brandeis Letters, supra note 3, at 138. The full story of Brandeis's involvement in developing the University of Louisville is told in Bernard Flexner, Mr. Justice Brandeis and the University of Louisville (1938).

8. Letter from Louis D. Brandeis to Otto A. Wehle (Mar. 12, 1876), in 1 Brandeis Letters, supra note 3, at 7.

9. Id.

10. Id.

11. See Letter from Louis D. Brandeis to Susan Brandeis (Nov. 15, 1916) (on file with the Gilbert Family Papers, Brandeis University Library, Waltham, Massachusetts).

12. See James Willard Hurst, The Growth of American Law: The Law Makers 311 (1950); Mason, supra note 6, at 640.

13. See Melvin I. Urofsky, A Mind of One Piece: Brandeis and American Reform 33-39 (1971).

14. See Oliver Wendell Holmes, Jr., The Common Law (1881).

15. See Letter from Louis D. Brandeis to John Hinkley (July 20, 1905), in 1 Brandeis Letters, supra note 3, at 338.

16. Louis D. Brandeis, The Opportunity in the Law, 39 Am. L. Rev. 555, 559-60 (1905).

17. See Melvin I. Urofsky, Louis D. Brandeis and the Progressive Tradition 47-67 (1981), for a discussion on Brandeis's reputation as an attorney concerned for people, rather than corporations.

18. See Philippa Strum, Louis D. Brandeis: Justice for the People 114-31 (1984), for development of the Brandeis brief in Muller v. Oregon, 208 U.S. 412 (1908).

19. See Strum, supra note 18, at 114-31.

20. See Mason, supra note 6, at 232-37.

21. See Edward F. McClennan, Louis D. Brandeis as a Lawyer, Mass. L.Q., Sept. 1948, at 2 (McClennan was Brandeis's law partner from the 1890s until Brandeis went onto the Supreme Court in 1916).

22. See David W. Levy, The Lawyer as Judge: Brandeis' View of the Legal Profession, 22 Okla. L. Rev. 374 (1969).

23. Id. at 389.

24. See Letter from Louis D. Brandeis to Adele Brandeis (Sept. 24, 1924), in 5 Brandeis Letters, supra note 3, at 138.

25. Letter from Louis D. Brandeis to Alfred Brandeis (Feb. 18, 1925), in 5 Brandeis Letters, supra note 3, at 163-64.
26. Letter from Louis D. Brandeis to Felix Frankfurter (Apr. 23, 1922), in Half Brother, supra note 4, at 100.
27. Id.
28. Id.
29. See Arthur E. Sutherland, The Law at Harvard: A History of Ideas and Men 1817-1967, at 262-70 (1967).
30. Letter from Louis D. Brandeis to Felix Frankfurter (Oct. 9, 1924), in Half Brother, supra note 4, at 175.
31. See Letter from Louis D. Brandeis to Felix Frankfurter (Oct. 25, 1924), in Half Brother, supra note 4, at 176.
32. See Flexner, supra note 7, for a discussion on Brandeis s connection with and support of the University of Louisville.
33. Proverbs 22:1.

Justice Brandeis's personal typewriter, one of the items in the Brandeis papers collection.

The Brandeis School of Law in 2006:
Carrying Out the Vision

Laura Rothstein
Dean (2000-2005)
Louis D. Brandeis School of Law
University of Louisville

One hundred fifty years after his birth, the law school named for Louis D. Brandeis carries out his vision in a number of ways.

Justice Brandeis believed in public service, and he gave substantial service himself. In 1990, the University of Louisville's law school became one of the first law schools in the country to adopt a mandatory public service program, cultivating an ethic of service. This program serves as a model for other law schools. Alums of the law school carry on the ethic of service after graduation, by giving their pro bono time to a number of programs that provide legal services to individuals who would not be represented otherwise.

Justice Brandeis believed that law is shaped significantly by social and economic forces, as exemplified in his "Brandeis Briefs." Today, the Brandeis School of Law offers five dual degree programs (business, social work, divinity, political science, and humanities). The teaching and scholarship of many faculty members crosses disciplines ranging from intellectual property to criminal justice to health policy.

Justice Brandeis believed that a law school should be a laboratory of innovation in public policy and an active force in the community. The Brandeis School of Law is involved in a number of partnerships with the Metro Louisville government promoting such innovations. Faculty members are actively involved in policy matters and a number of partnership projects at the local, state, national, and international levels.

Justice Brandeis thought it important to honor and recognize the history of Kentucky. The law school has followed the example of honoring history through its recent renovation projects. Classroom renovations in recent years have honored and recognized the contributions of Wilson Wyatt, Sr., the history of women in law in Kentucky, and the 1950s era (which included return of soldiers, merger of the Jefferson School of Law, the emergence of the oral advocacy program, and desegregation of the university and the law school). Following the example of Justice Brandeis, who provided funds for the maintenance of the law school, numerous alums and friends have contributed their resources to making these renovations possible.

It was a Brandeis philosophy that a law school should be small and collegial. The Brandeis School of Law has an enrollment of just over 400 students, with 33 faculty members. As a result, the law school has one of the most favorable student faculty ratios in the country, and most classes are small, allowing the students and faculty to know each other well.

Justice Brandeis was an outstanding advocate—both through his writings and his advocacy in court and before policymaking agencies. The Brandeis School of Law exemplifies an excellent program of advocacy through the Lively M. Wilson Oral Advocacy Program. Through the program, students participate in about 15 national and regional oral advocacy competitions each year covering areas of law that include environmental, securities, health, tax, trademark, labor, criminal, trial advocacy, negotiation, client counseling and more. Students at the Brandeis School of Law have a long list of victories in those competitions.

One of the areas to which Justice Brandeis gave attention as a practicing lawyer and advocate was labor and employment issues. The "Brandeis Brief" is about women's working hours. He was concerned about the safety of workers. He advocated for policies for regularity of work. In 1984, Dean Barbara Lewis initiated the first annual Carl A. Warns Jr. Labor and Employment Law Institute. The annual conference brings an exemplary group of speakers each year to the two day conference, which balances academic and practical perspectives on current important labor and employment issues.

Justice Brandeis's academic record at Harvard Law School remains the highest of any law graduate. In 1976 the Brandeis Honor Society was founded by law students, faculty and administrators to honor students who demonstrate excellence in their legal studies. These students are recognized each year at the dinner where the Brandeis Medal is presented. At the event, a student member, selected from the society, is given the high honor of introducing the Brandeis Medal Recipient.

The American Inns of Court program was established in the United States in 1985, and was modeled after the English Inns of Court. The Inns' purpose is to "improve the skills, professionalism and legal ethics of the bench and bar" by establishing a "society of judges, lawyers, legal educators, law students and others to promote excellence in legal advocacy." In 1995, the Louis D. Brandeis American Inn of Court was established. It has approximately 80 members, 12 of whom are law students. This interaction of students with members of bench and bar is a tribute to the Brandeis philosophy that the legal profession and law schools should be collegial.

The use of research found in law review articles was of great value to Justice

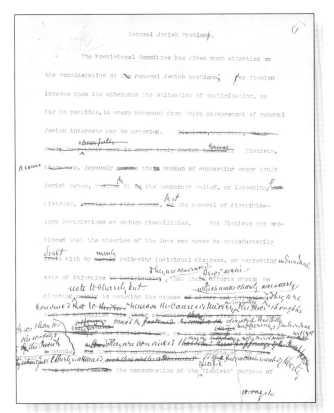

This document from the Brandeis Papers collection demonstrates the meticulous editing style of Justice Brandeis.

Brandeis. In 1997, the law review at the University of Louisville, which had previously been called the Journal of Family Law, was renamed the Brandeis Law Journal. This reflects the broader substantive coverage of the journal. In the years since the name change, the Brandeis Law Journal has published numerous outstanding articles by highly recognized scholars, as well as provided an outlet for high quality student writing.

In an Inaugural Volume Dedication of the Brandeis Law Journal, two of his grandchildren, Alice Brandeis Popkin and Frank Brandeis Gilbert wrote the following:

> Our grandfather, Louis D. Brandeis, would feel honored by the naming of the School of Law at the University of Louisville in his memory and would be pleased that the Brandeis Law Journal demonstrates the law school's commitment to excellence and breadth in legal information.
>
> The Brandeis Law Journal will provide a forum for scholarly research of the facts and legal concepts involved in a given situation, following Grandfather's approach to legal problem solving. Grandfather always took the time to master all of the facts compressing a legal issue. When he was a private attorney, he submitted—and the Supreme Court accepted and used—his brief in *Muller v. Oregon*. It contained two pages of legal arguments and more than one hundred pages referring to factual reports and existing laws affecting the parties involved. This "Brandeis Brief" is an example of the creative approach to legal issues that the Brandeis Law Journal and the interdisciplinary courses at the law school will hopefully foster.
>
> Grandfather's mastery of the law combined an understanding of the facts with a dedication to researching the complete background and history of any legal question. His commitment to research permeated his work on the Supreme Court, as his law clerks discovered during long hours spent at the Library of Congress. Grandfather's dedication to his work on the Court was visible through his actions. Even during his summer vacation in Chatham, Massachusetts, he rose early each morning to read petitions for certiorari in his plain study attached to the house. Grandfather corrected— in his own unmistakable handwriting—the many printed drafts of each Supreme Court opinion. At times, the Brandeis Law Journal editors may want to refer to his reported statement that "there is no such thing as good writing, only good legal rewriting."
>
> In 1905, Grandfather said, "there is a call upon the legal profession to do great work for this country." [Louis D. Brandeis, The Opportunity in the Law, 39 Am. L. Rev. 555, 563 (1905)] The Louis D. Brandeis School of Law is carrying out many of the ideas and policies identified with Grandfather. As the fifty states introduce new programs relating to the environment, welfare, and other fields people often refer to his concept that the states may become laboratories of democracy and "try novel social and economic experiments without risk to the rest of the country." The University of Louisville, as a state institution, has played a role in the implementation of this concept.

The ideas and research of the law school's faculty and students have proven a valuable resource for the city, county, and state governments in Kentucky.

A valuable feature of the law school is its mandatory public service program—a tie-in to Grandfather's extensive involvement with public issues while in private practice. His work on behalf of people who were underrepresented earned him the description, "the people's attorney." President Wilson spoke warmly of Grandfather's public service activities at the time that the Senate debated his nomination to the Supreme Court.

In this inaugural volume…we should mention Grandfather's active involvement as an alumnus in the early years of the Harvard Law Review and his twenty-five year service as a Harvard Law School Trustee. An article he co-authored in an early issue of the Harvard Law Review gave him his first opportunity to argue for the establishment of a "right to privacy." [See Samuel D. Warren & Louis D. Brandeis, The Right to Privacy, 4 Harv. L. Rev. 193 (1890).]

Grandfather cared deeply for the University of Louisville and its service to the city of his birth. Writing to his brother in Louisville in 1925, he spoke about his hopes for the University. "To become great, a University must express the people whom it serves and must express the people and the community at their best. The aim must be high and the vision broad; the goal seemingly unattainable but beyond immediate reach." Grandfather would be pleased the University and the School of Law, in part through the Brandeis Law Journal, are today aiming high and have attained goals that, seventy-five years ago, were beyond their reach.

—"*A Letter from Grandchildren of Justice Louis D. Brandeis," Alice Brandeis Popkin and Frank Brandeis Gilbert. 37 Brandeis Law Journal 173 (1998-99). Mrs. Popkin is a lawyer practicing in Chatham, Massachusetts. Mr. Gilbert is a lawyer serving as senior field representative at the National Trust for Historic Preservation, Washington, D.C.*

Students and visitors to the law school are frequently reminded of the Brandeis vision, through our programs, publications, and displays. We are proud to be known as the Brandeis School of Law and proud that we carry out his vision in so many of our programs and activities.

Knowledge is Essential...

This mosaic created by Harold Berg for the law school includes one of the many well-known quotes of Justice Brandeis. The mosaic is displayed in the foyer of the classroom wing at the Brandeis School of Law, reminding students, faculty, staff, and visitors of the wisdom of the person for whom the law school is named.

"KNOWLEDGE IS ESSENTIAL TO UNDERSTANDING AND UNDERSTANDING SHOULD PRECEDE JUDGING"

JUSTICE LOUIS D. BRANDEIS

Louis D. Brandeis

His Family and His Life Before Harvard

Leslie Abramson
Frost Brown Todd Professor of Law
Louis D. Brandeis School of Law

The name "Brandeis" is found on Prague tombstones dating to 1539. The Brandeises of Prague included squires, land owners, rabbis, and martyrs. The Dembitz family name is traceable to Dr. Dembitz who as a young student in 1792 Prague joined the Frankist movement, named for Jacob Frank who proclaimed himself a prophet and the messiah of the Jewish people.

Adolph Brandeis arrived in America in the fall of 1848 at age twenty-six. His journey's purpose was to investigate America's opportunities for himself and several families in Prague, then a part of Bohemia (and later Germany). Jews in Prague were subject to growing governmental restrictions on their activities and an 1848 revolution had failed.

On his trip to America, Adolph left behind his twenty-year-old fiancée, Frederika Dembitz, who spoke several languages and was an accomplished pianist. She arrived (with more than twenty others) in New York the following spring. Adolph moved them to Cincinnati where he had rented a four-story house. Soon, most of the new immigrants moved to Madison, Indiana, where they established a successful grocery and produce store. Adolph and Frederika married there on September 5, 1849. Within a year, their first child Fanny was born, named for Frederika's mother.

Sensing that Madison was not growing, Adolph and Frederika soon moved to Louisville, Kentucky. The cultural atmosphere in the Brandeis home was German, which was the spoken language, as well as the dominant theme of music, art and literature there. More than half of Louisville's foreign-born population in the

Eric Tachau and Jean Haas, descendants of Alfred Brandeis (brother of Louis Brandeis) gave the law school brass relief portraits of Brandeis's father, Adolph, and his sister, Fannie. These are displayed in the Handmaker Room, in the University of Louisville Louis D. Brandeis School of Law library along with the Brandeis papers.

mid-nineteenth century was German, like the Brandeis family.

In Louisville, Adolph operated a flour mill, a tobacco factory, an 1,100 acre farm, and a steam freighter called the Fanny Brandeis. After the birth of Fanny, Amy arrived in 1852, followed by her brother Alfred in 1854. Louis Dembitz Brandeis was born there on November 13, 1856. As the youngest of four children, Louis grew up in a household that was tolerant of both Jewish and Christian rituals.

Louis David Brandeis was named for his mother's brother, Lewis N. Dembitz, who was a lawyer and abolitionist, and one of three nominators of Abraham Lincoln at the Chicago National Republican Convention of 1860. As a sign of his high regard for his uncle, Louis later adopted his uncle's surname as his middle name. His uncle remained an intellectual mentor after Louis moved to Boston.

Louis recalled years later that his earliest memories were of his mother serving food and coffee to Union soldiers. The family briefly moved across the Ohio River to Indiana when Confederate armies threatened to attack Louisville in the fall of 1862. Adolph's shipping contracts with the government improved the family's economic fortunes during the Civil War. The family moved from a house on First Street to a large limestone house on Broadway. Despite the war, the family also took trips to places like Niagara Falls and Newport, Rhode Island.

Louis excelled in his studies, compiling an outstanding scholastic record at the German and English Academy and at Male High School in Louisville. His Academy principal awarded him a special commendation for his conduct and hard work. In 1872, at the age of sixteen, the Louisville University of the Public Schools awarded Louis a gold medal for "pre-eminence in all his studies."

By then, Adolph's business began to decline because his southern customers could not pay their bills. He dissolved his businesses and took the family to Europe. Louis tried to enter the Gymnasium in Vienna to continue his formal education, but was unable to pass the entrance examinations. He nevertheless spent the academic year traveling and taking university courses. In 1873, he tried to enroll in Dresden, Germany at the Annen-Realschule. The school rector told him that he could not be admitted without proof of

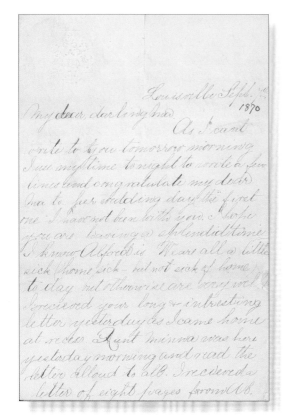

This letter to Brandeis's mother, which is included in the Brandeis Papers collection, was written when he was 12 years old and is the earliest example of his writing still extant. The text of the letter can be found on page 3 of Volume I of The Letters of Louis D. Brandeis, 5 volumes, *edited by Melvin I. Urofsky and David W. Levy.*

birth and the necessary vaccinations. Louis responded, "The fact that I'm here is proof of my birth, and you may look at my arm for evidence that I was vaccinated." The startled rector permitted Louis to enroll, and he studied there for three terms. Later, he credited his Dresden experience for teaching him how to think analytically.

Returning to America in 1875, Louis was determined to follow in his Uncle Lewis's footsteps and become an attorney. At the age of eighteen, he was admitted to Harvard Law School without preliminary college training. Harvard authorities suspended the required age rules so that Louis could graduate and earn his degree with record-breaking grades before he was 21 in 1877.

Although he never returned to Louisville to live, he visited and remained in close contact with family members through frequent correspondence. In particular, he corresponded with his mother, his brother (Alfred), and his uncle Lewis Dembitz. He retained a strong interest in the University of Louisville and the law school throughout his life.

Bibliography

Jacob De Haas, Louis D. Brandeis: A Biographical Sketch, (Block Publishing Company 1929)

Allon Gal, Brandeis of Boston, (Harvard University Press 1980)

Lewis J. Paper, Brandeis, (Prentice-Hall 1983)

Philippa Strum, Louis D. Brandeis: Justice for the People, (Harvard University Press 1984)

Justice Brandeis' brother Alfred (1854–1928) remained in Louisville and joined their father Adolph in the grain merchant business Brandeis and Son. Alfred became a socially prominent citizen who was a member of the Board of Trade of Louisville as well as a director of a number of banks. He had four daughters, three of whom carried on the Brandeis tradition of public service.

Adele Brandeis (1885–1975), daughter of Alfred Brandeis, worked as an arts supervisor for the Kentucky WPA (Works Progress Administration) and as an editorial writer for the Louisville Courier-Journal. In 1949, she became the first woman trustee of the University of Louisville.

Fanny Brandeis (1892–1971), daughter of Alfred Brandeis, was one of the founders of the Louisville Orchestra and was the supervisor of the Federal Music Project in Kentucky during the 1930s. Both Fanny and Adele were active helpers in Justice Brandeis' improvement plans for the University of Louisville.

Jean Brandeis Tachau (1894–1978), daughter of Alfred Brandeis, helped create the Kentucky Birth Control League in 1933 and in the 1940s became the chair of the Child Welfare Division of the Health and Welfare Council in Louisville. In the 1960s she became involved in the struggle to ensure open housing for African-Americans in Louisville. Her sons, Charles Tachau and Eric Tachau (both actively involved in issues of social justice), were both graduates of the University of Louisville law school, thus bringing Brandeis' connection to the law school back to the family.

Brandeis canoeing on the Potomac, May 1919.

Brandeis in Nature

Justice Brandeis, although he worked long hours, believed strongly in having meaningful leisure. This meant both time to relax and reflect at the end of the day and time each year for vacation. He believed such time was essential to refresh one's mind. One of his many famous quotes is:

"I can do twelve months work in eleven months, but not in twelve."

Some of the most unique images of Justice Brandeis in the papers collection are from a large scrapbook of his 1885 camping trip with friends during the time he was a practicing lawyer. Although he is "on vacation" and wearing camping clothes, he is nonetheless still wearing a tie. The photo of him canoeing on the Potomac also depicts his formal attire even while relaxing.

His love of getting out into nature—by canoeing, traveling to the Canadian forests, and riding horses—developed early in his life. The advocacy work of Justice Brandeis on conservation occurred in three places. First, in 1910 he defended conservation in connection with the alleged selling of western natural resources to the Guggenheim corporation, in opposition to the preservation and conservation policies of the Theodore Roosevelt administration. He later advised about the exploitation of Alaskan natural resources. During the Franklin Roosevelt administration, he thought conservation projects would be an excellent way to fight unemployment during the Great Depression.

References: Volume II, *The Letters of Louis D. Brandeis*, edited by Melvin I. Urofsky and David W. Levy, pp. 467-474; and *The Family Letters of Louis D. Brandeis*, edited by Melvin I. Urofsky and David W. Levy, pp. 533-534.

The Brandeis Brief

In 1908 Brandeis submitted to the Supreme Court a brief that changed the course of American legal history. The occasion was a case called *Muller v. Oregon.* With only a few sentences connecting hundreds of pages of supporting statistics, Brandeis argued for the constitutionality of a state law limiting working hours.

The technique worked. The Court upheld the law and specifically credited Brandeis and his approach. Brandeis had managed to create an entry to the Court for social facts.

The impact of *Muller* was tremendous.

Brandeis was so insistent that intelligent action could follow only after accumulation of facts that the approach was a completely logical one for him, but it was not at all the norm in American law. As he said, "In the past the courts have reached their conclusions largely deductively from preconceived notions and precedents. The method I have tried to apply in arguing cases before them has been inductive, reasoning from the facts."

This was the new sociological jurisprudence espoused by Brandeis. To find out what a law means one must first find out what it should mean, given the current needs of society. Thus, judges had to base their decisions on facts.

> —From *Louis D. Brandeis, Justice for the People* (pages 114, 122, 124-125), by Philippa Strum

The "Brandeis Brief" technique was adopted by others, and was later used in one of the most important Supreme Court decisions of the 20th century—*Brown v. Board of Education.* The NAACP used Justice Brandeis' social science methods in the school desegregation cases leading up to and including *Brown.* The stigma and the psychological damage to black children excluded from white schools was presented as evidence in the five cases consolidated before the Supreme Court. The evidence was persuasive, and the Court finally overruled as unconstitutional the concept of separate but equal, which had been established in the 1896 *Plessy v. Ferguson* decision. Only Justice John Marshall Harlan had dissented in that decision.

Justice Brandeis also played a key role in the story of *Brown* in a less well known way. When Mordecai Johnson became President of Howard University in 1926, he knew that vast improvements were needed. "In one area, he was told there was a special need for swift and drastic overhaul—the law school. And Mordecai Johnson listened because the man who told him was Louis Brandeis, Associate Justice of the Supreme Court of the United States." [Simple Justice, by Richard Kluger, 2nd edition 2004] As a result of this advice, new faculty were brought to the law school. Thurgood Marshall (later Supreme Court Justice) came to Howard Law School in 1930, and worked along with Charles Houston and others in developing the NAACP civil rights case leading up to *Brown*, and subsequent school integration cases, using law and social science in the way first developed in the Brandeis Brief.

Thurgood Marshall, counsel for the National Association for the Advancement of Colored People, in the lawyer's lounge after presenting the NAACP's case to the Supreme Court in the momentous Little Rock school integration case. September 11, 1958, Washington, DC. Photo courtesy of Bettmann/CORBIS.

The Brandeis Papers

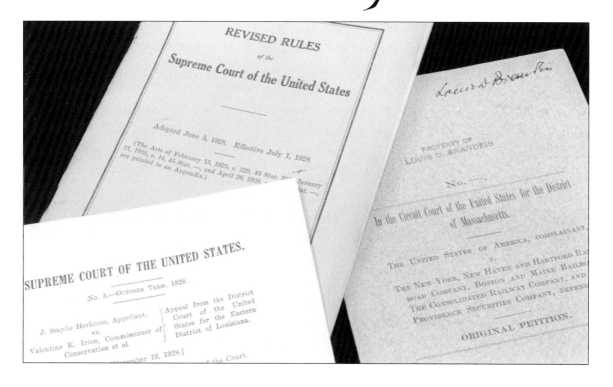

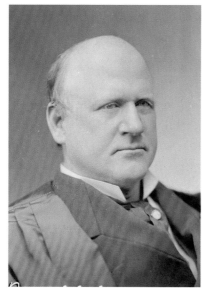

Justice John Marshall Harlan followed Brandeis's lead by donating nearly 8,000 items from his library to the law school.

Information from documents prepared by Donald L. Burnett, Jr., Peter Scott Campbell, Linda Ewald, Barbara Lewis, Kurt Metzmeier, and Laura Rothstein.

One of the most significant gifts of Justice Brandeis to the University of Louisville Law School was his personal library (including many rare texts on early civil and common law) and his personal papers (comprising approximately 250,000 items). The gift of the papers followed a conversation between Neville N. Miller (Dean of the Law School) and Justice Brandeis during a visit to Cape Cod.

Justice Brandeis also aided the law school in obtaining the papers of Justice John Marshall Harlan (the "great dissenter"). Justice Harlan's papers include approximately 8,000 items. Scrapbooks kept by Mrs. Harlan were of particular interest to Supreme Court Justice Ruth Bader Ginsburg during her 2003 visit to the law school, because of Justice Ginsburg's efforts to see the publication of the memoirs of Mrs. Harlan—"Some Memories of a Long Life, 1854–1911," by Malvina Shanklin Harlan. Harlan's scrapbooks also included newspaper clippings about Justice Harlan after he wrote his famous dissent in *Plessy v. Ferguson*.

Justice Brandeis also arranged for the law school to receive original briefs filed with the United States Supreme Court. At the time of the first donation in the 1920s, only twenty institutions received such briefs. These briefs include those from the *Brown v. Board of Education* decision, a case in which the plaintiffs used the Brandeis Brief methodology of including economic and social science research to argue the case.

The personal papers of Justice Brandeis are now housed in the Handmaker Room in the law library at the Brandeis School of Law. The room includes Brandeis' original appointment and retirement documents, photos of the Supreme Court during his service, books from his Boston law office, rare books in Latin on the civil law, and a rare set of "Blackstone's Commentaries" on the common law. The typewriter is the one he used to compose many of America's most famous judicial opinions. Also in the collection is Justice Brandeis' grade-school reading primer.

The collection of more than a quarter million items includes donations from Justice Brandeis, his family, Alphus Mason, and Brandeis' former law firm (Nutter, McClellen and Fish). The room was furnished with funds provided by the Handmaker family of Louisville.

The papers cover nearly every aspect of Brandeis' life, most notably Zionism, World War I, the creation of savings bank life insurance, the University of Louisville, the Boston and Maine/New Haven Railroad merger, and correspondence with family, friends, and leading intellectuals of the day. The only aspects not covered extensively are his life before his legal career, and material relating to the cases he heard while on the Supreme Court.

The Brandeis and Harlan papers have been used by many scholars. Available on microfilm, through the work of Tom Owen, University of Louisville Archivist, a guide to the collection is available on http://www.law.louisville.edu/library/brandeis. The Temple, Louisville's oldest and largest synagogue, dedicated an archive center in 2003, and it includes some letters from Justice Brandeis to a cousin living in Jerusalem.

The Art of Brandeis

This section is adapted from an article by David Ensign, Dean of the Brandeis School of Law, entitled "The Art of Brandeis," published in the January 2006 Louisville Bar Association Bar Briefs.

The law school has several significant works of art depicting Justice Brandeis. These include two etchings by William Meyerowitz, depicting Justice Brandeis in his later years, and an Andy Warhol portrait. The Warhol portrait is one of 200 in a numbered print silk screen issue, and is part of a series titled *Ten Portraits of Jews of the Twentieth Century*. A 3-1/2 by 5-1/2 inch postcard with an oval picture of Brandeis on the front is part of the papers collection. Text in Hebrew printed on the front of the card reads, "Louis Brandeis first president of Israel Hanukah 5679." A message on the back of the card is written in Russian or Bulgarian from someone named Sara, but the card was never mailed. The text is dated December 18, 1917 and reads, "Congratulations on the new state." Apparently it is a reference to speculation that Brandeis would be named President of a new Zionist state.

Etching by William Meyerowitz, printed with permission of the William and Theresa Meyerowitz Foundation.

During his life and career, Justice Brandeis is known to have sat for only one painted portrait. At the time he was only 32, a young Boston attorney, with his great years of fame ahead. The portrait was painted in 1888 by Frank H. Tompkins at the request of Brandeis' brother, Alfred. The large oil painting was a 2002 gift from members of the Brandeis family: the children of Susan Brandeis (Brandeis' daughter)—Louis B. Gilbert, Alice B. Popkin and Frank B. Gilbert—and Alice's daughters Susan B. Cahn, Anne B. Popkin and Louisa B. Popkin.

One of the more whimsical artworks is a poster of a pop art piece titled *Louis D. Brandeis on Democracy* by James Rosenquist. It is an interpretation of a Brandeis quotation.

Portrait painted by Frank H. Tompkins, 1888. Donated to the law school by family members in 2002.

The quotation is represented by one automobile door colliding with another automobile door in a bed of Franco-American spaghetti. It says, "That margin between that which men naturally do and that which they can do is so great that a system which urges men to action and develops individual enterprise and initiative is preferable in spite of the wastes that necessarily attend that process."

An image that is regularly used in law school publications is from a mosaic created by Dr. Harold Berg which is displayed in the classroom wing foyer area. The mosaic of the Blindfolded Lady Justice holding the scales of justice is surrounded by a Brandeis quote— "Knowledge is essential to understanding and understanding should precede judging." This work of art is a daily reminder of the wisdom of Justice Brandeis.

In 2000, Jean Haas (granddaughter of Alfred Brandeis, older brother of Justice Brandeis), gave a brass relief portrait of Brandeis' father, Adolph. In 2001, the late Eric Tachau (grandson of Alfred Brandeis) gave a brass relief of Brandeis' sister, Fannie.

The Brandeis Medal

The Brandeis Medal was established to recognize individuals whose lives reflect Justice Brandeis' commitment to the ideals of individual liberty, concern for the disadvantaged, and public service. The medal itself is cast in the likeness of Justice Brandeis as a reminder of his contributions and dedication to the law. It was awarded for the first time in 1982.

The following are the recipients and a summary of their major accomplishments at the time they received the Brandeis Medal.

Shirley Hufstedler
Judge, Ninth Circuit Court of Appeals
Secretary of Education
Awarded the Medal in 1982

Shirley Hufstedler served on the Ninth Circuit Court of Appeals from 1968 to 1980. In 1979, she was named by President Jimmy Carter to be the first Secretary of Education, to serve when the Department of Education was established in 1980. She received her undergraduate degree in business administration from the University of New Mexico and her law degree from Stanford University. She was the second woman to become a federal appellate judge. Before her service at the federal level, she engaged in private practice and served as a county and state law judge.

After leaving the Department of Education, she returned to private practice and teaching. She is currently Senior Counsel at Morrison and Foerster in Los Angeles.

Portrait of Justice and Mrs. Blackmun at the portico. A tradition when a Supreme Court Justice visits the law school is the laying of a wreath at the gravesite of Justice Brandeis.

Harry Blackmun
Associate Justice of the U.S. Supreme Court
Awarded the Medal in 1983

Justice Blackmun was appointed to the Supreme Court in 1970 and served until his retirement from the Court in 1994. He attended Harvard College, graduating with a degree in mathematics before receiving his law degree at Harvard. He was engaged in private practice specializing in tax law and estate planning before his appointment to the Eighth Circuit Court of Appeals in 1959, and his later appointment to the Supreme Court by President Richard Nixon. He became renowned while on the Court for his opinions on tax cases. His tenure was marked by his opposition to capital punishment and his advocacy for individual rights. He wrote the majority opinion in *Roe v. Wade*.

Justice Blackmun died in 1999, five years after leaving the Court.

Charles Allen
Senior District Judge, Western District of Kentucky
Awarded the Medal in 1985

A 1943 graduate of the Louis D. Brandeis School of Law, Judge Allen distinguished himself in the practice of law in both private practice and as Assistant U.S. Attorney. He was selected to the chancery division of the Jefferson County Circuit Court in 1961, and in 1971 was nominated by President Nixon to serve as a federal judge on the Western District of Kentucky, where he served in various capacities, including Chief Judge and Senior District Judge. He was known as an advocate for economic, social, and political justice. His work included desegregation of the Louisville police department, ending the practice of warehousing mentally ill individuals, and altering inhumane prison conditions.

Judge Allen died on January 4, 2000. He was serving as Senior District Judge of the Western District of Kentucky at the time of his death. Judge Allen was recognized by the law school as the Law Alumni Fellow in 1991.

Christopher Dodd
United States Senator
Awarded the Medal in 1986

Senator Dodd is a 1972 graduate of the Louis D. Brandeis School of Law. He began his service in the United States Senate in 1980, and has a long and distinguished record of leadership on issues relating to health, education, labor, banking, housing, and urban affairs. He also has a strong record in areas of environmental protection, foreign policy, housing and economic development. He organized the Senate Children's Caucus to focus attention on issues affecting children. His record of achievement and leadership and respect among his peers was acknowledged in 1983, when he was awarded a Doctor of Law (Honoris Causa) in 1984.

In 2001, Senator Dodd was selected as the law school's 2001 Alumni Fellow.

John S. Palmore
Chief Justice, Kentucky Supreme Court
Awarded the Medal in 1987

Chief Justice Palmore is a graduate of Western Kentucky University and the Brandeis School of Law. After law school he served in private practice, to which he returned after serving in the U.S. Navy during World War II. He was elected as City Prosecuting Attorney, and then served in the Navy during the Korean Conflict, returning again to private practice. After service as City Attorney and Commonwealth Attorney in Henderson, Kentucky, he was elected to the Court of Appeals (later renamed the Supreme Court of Kentucky) in 1959. He was re-elected and continued service until his retirement in 1983. He served as Chief Justice in 1966, 1974, and 1977-1982. His leadership on the court brought about significant improvements in Kentucky criminal law and improving the state court system to today's modern system of courts.

Justice Palmore has also been honored by the Brandeis School of Law with the Grauman Award and the Law Alumni Fellow Award in 1993.

Morris Dees
Cofounder, Southern Poverty Law Center
Awarded the Medal in 1991

The son of an Alabama farmer, Morris Dees was a firsthand witness to prejudice and racial injustice. Mr. Dees graduated from the University of Alabama School of Law in 1960, after which he practiced law and developed a successful book publishing business. In 1967 he began taking controversial cases unpopular among the white community, and this experience led him to become a cofounder of the Southern Poverty Law Center in 1971. The Center focuses on suing hate groups and on other issues addressing equal opportunities for minorities and the poor.

Sandra Day O'Connor
Associate Justice of the U.S. Supreme Court
Awarded the Medal in 1992

Justice O'Connor was appointed to the Supreme Court by President Ronald Reagan in 1981. While serving on the Supreme Court, Justice O'Connor maintained her interest in improving the legal profession, including public service. She received both her B.A. and J.D. from Stanford University, and her legal career has encompassed the roles of practitioner, legislator, trial judge, state appellate judge, and Justice of the United States Supreme Court. From 1952 to 1969, she engaged in private practice and held several public positions, including Deputy County Attorney in San Mateo County, California, and Assistant Attorney General for the State of Arizona. From 1969 to 1975 she served three terms in the Arizona State Senate. During the third term she was elected Senate Majority Leader. Her judicial service began in 1975, when she was elected judge of the Maricopa County Superior Court and in 1979 she was appointed to the Arizona Court of Appeals. She has been a voice of moderation on the Supreme Court, her opinions being key to a number of close decisions on important social issues.

Justice O'Connor returned to the law school to give a talk on her book, "Majesty of the Court," as part of the Kentucky Author Forum in May 2003. She resigned from the Court effective in 2006.

Leon Higginbotham, Jr.
Chief Judge, Third Circuit Court of Appeals
Awarded the Medal in 1994

A graduate of Antioch College and Yale Law School, Judge Higginbotham was appointed as district court judge in 1964, and Judge of the Third Circuit Court of Appeals in 1977. He served in a number of other governmental and public service positions including vice chairman of the National Commission on the Causes and Prevention of Violence, judicial conference committees, and as a commissioner of the Federal Trade Commission from 1962 to 1964. His scholarship focused on matters of race, and he taught as an adjunct professor at several law schools.

Judge Higginbotham died in 1998.

Robert M. Morgenthau
New York District Attorney
Awarded the Medal in 1995

A graduate of Amherst College and Yale Law School, Robert Morgenthau is known as a public servant and prosecutor in cases involving corruption, racketeering and white collar crime. His is also an active advocate of victim's rights. After graduation from law school, he was in private practice for thirteen years in New York City before being appointed by President Kennedy to be United States Attorney for the Southern District of New York. High profile cases have included kickbacks in New York City government contracts, price manipulation of American Stock Exchange listings, bribery in the Manhattan IRS office, and abuse of Swiss bank accounts by corporate officers.

Archibald Cox
Watergate Prosecutor
Harvard Law Professor
Awarded the Medal in 1996

Archibald Cox is best known for his role in the Watergate investigation, when he served as the first special prosecutor named in that investigation. He was appointed by Attorney General Elliot L. Richardson in 1973, and was ultimately fired by Solicitor General Robert H. Bork, in what is known as the "Saturday Night Massacre"because of the controversy surrounding his termination. A graduate of Harvard College and Harvard Law School, he engaged in private practice followed by service on the Harvard Law School faculty before the Watergate events. After Watergate, he worked with Common Cause, an advocacy group working on behalf of campaign finance reform and ethics laws, and he taught law school at Harvard and Boston University. His scholarship includes exemplary works in labor law and constitutional law.

Archibald Cox died in 2004.

Charles Ogletree
Harvard Law Professor
Awarded the Medal in 1997

In a legal career bridging the academy and the profession, Charles Ogletree has established a reputation for rigorous constitutional scholarship, a commitment to equal justice under law, and a record of public service. Professor Ogletree received a B.A. and M.A. from Stanford and his law degree from Harvard. After practice in the Public Defender Service in Washington DC and private practice in Washington, he joined the Harvard law faculty as a full time faculty member in 1989, where he teaches criminal law and related topics. His is an active scholar on topics of constitutional law, criminal law and procedure, and equal justice.

Stephen Bright
Director,
Southern Center for Human Rights
Awarded the Medal in 1998

A Kentucky native, Stephen Bright is Director (since 1982) of the Southern Center for Human Rights, a public interest legal project based in Atlanta, which provides representation to persons facing the death penalty and to prisoners challenging unconstitutional conditions in prisons and jails. A graduate of the University of Kentucky School of Law, he has taught courses on capital punishment, criminal procedure, international human rights laws and prisoners' rights at several law schools and has written extensively on the death penalty and other topics. Following the Brandeis model of advocacy before government entities, he has testified before Congressional Committees and state committees on capital punishment, and has influenced policy in this area.

Stephen Bright delivered the 2002 law school commencement address, and at that time he was given an honorary degree from the University of Louisville.

Abner Mikva
U.S. Court of Appeals, White House Counsel
Awarded the Medal in 1999

Judge Mikva served as Chief Judge on the United States Court of Appeals for the District of Columbia from 1979 to 1994 (1991-1994 as Chief Judge). A graduate of the University of Chicago School of Law, he practiced law, presenting several constitutional cases to the Supreme Court, before serving in Illinois House of Representatives for five terms and Congress for five terms. During his time in the Illinois House, he helped enact a new criminal code and a new mental health code for Illinois. His service in the legislative and judicial branches of government was rounded out through his service in the administrative branch, as White House Counsel from October 1, 1994 until November 1, 1995. He has taught law at a number of law schools and has written numerous tests on the legislative process.

John Lewis
Member, U.S. House of Representatives
Awarded the Medal in 2000

Congressman John Lewis (Georgia) has demonstrated a lifelong commitment to human rights, preservation of personal dignity, and unfailing support of social justice, and one of the most courageous persons in the Civil Rights Movement. With degrees from Fisk University, the American Baptist Theological Seminary in Nashville, he was first elected to the U.S. House of Representatives in 1986, and has served in many leadership positions. He began his commitment as a college student, organizing peaceful sit-ins at segregated lunch counters, and participated at the risk of grave personal injury, in the 1961 "Freedom Rides" to protest segregated bus stations. As one of the "Big Six" leaders of the Civil Rights Movement, he helped to plan the historic August 1963 "March on Washington" and delivered a keynote address. His 1965 non-violent march into Selma, Alabama, and the ensuing police action laid the cornerstone for the Voting Rights Act of 1965. He was instrumental in registering more than four million minority voters. He was appointed by President Jimmy Carter to direct the federal volunteer agency known as ACTION.

Samuel Dash
Chief Counsel, Senate Watergate Committee
Georgetown University Law Professor
Awarded the Medal in 2001

Professor Dash captured the nation's attention as Chief Counsel to the Senate Watergate Committee from 1973 through 1974. With a B.S. from Temple University and a J.D. from Harvard Law School, he co-founded the Harvard Voluntary Defenders at Harvard. This is a still-thriving student clinical program created to provide legal assistance to indigent defendants. Following faculty service at Northwestern University School of Law, he served for several years in the Philadelphia District Attorney's Office, including appointment as District Attorney. During this time he wrote *The Eavesdroppers*, a book that helped change the law on electronic surveillance. This service was followed by eight years in private practice and two years as Director of the Philadelphia Council for Community Advancement and five years as Executive Director of the D.C. Judicial Conference Project on Mental Disorders.

He served as a member of the Georgetown Law Center faculty for many years until his death in 2004. He maintained an active courseload at the law school, and his lifelong pursuit of justice was a source of personal inspiration for his students and the legal profession.

Janet Reno
United States Attorney General
Awarded the Medal in 2002

The first female attorney general, Janet Reno's courage, vision, and dedication to professionalism and public service made her one of the country's most highly respected lawyers. During her eight year watch as Attorney General, crime was reduced dramatically and heightened professionalism became the order of the day in the law enforcement community. Attorney General Reno devoted substantial new resources to the development of information technology to combat crime. She also made issues relating to women and children high priorities, implementing the Violence Against Women Act of 1994. A graduate of Cornell University and Harvard Law School, she served as State's Attorney for Dade County, Florida, for 15 years before become Attorney General. She advocates the Brandeis value of an interdisciplinary approach to solving problems.

Ruth Bader Ginsburg
Associate Justice of the U.S. Supreme Court
Awarded the Medal in 2003

Justice Ginsburg became an Associate Justice of the United States Supreme Court in 1993, following service as a judge of the United States Court of Appeals for the District of Columbia from 1980 to 1993. She received her B.A. from Cornell University, attended Harvard Law School and received her law degree from Columbia Law School. She entered academic in 1963, serving on the law faculties at Rutgers University and Columbia Law School, where she was the first woman to hold a tenured professorship. She is known for her work to promote gender equality and civil rights. She co-founded the Women's Rights Project of the American Civil Liberties Union, and served as ACLU General Counsel from 1973 to 1980.

Stephen Breyer
Associate Justice of the
U.S. Supreme Court
Awarded the Medal in 2004

Justice Breyer became an Associate Justice of the Supreme Court of the United States in 1994, after serving as Chief Judge of the United States Court of Appeals for the First Circuit. A graduate of Stanford University, Oxford University (Magdalen College), and Harvard Law School, Justice Breyer enjoyed a long career as a Harvard law professor before service in the judiciary. He is known for his tenure as Assistant Special Prosecutor of the Watergate Special Prosecution Force, Chief Counsel of the U.S. Senate Judiciary Committee, and his work on the United States Sentencing Commission. His interest in economic regulation is articulated in his books *Regulation and Its Reform* and *Breaking the Vicious Circle: Toward Effective Risk Regulation*. His commitment to public service is demonstrated through his frequent participation in discussions and lectures on a variety of public policy subjects without compensation. Like Justice Brandeis, Justice Breyer advocated on issues of public interest such as utility regulation.

Howard Baker
United States Senator
White House Chief of Staff
Ambassador to Japan
Awarded the Medal in 2005

Senator Howard H. Baker first received national recognition in 1973 as the Vice Chairman of the Senate Watergate Committee. Although his most recent service in public life was as U.S. Ambassador to Japan (2001-2004), and he served as President Reagan's Chief of Staff from February 1987 until July 1988, he is most known for his service in the United States Senate. The first Republican ever popularly elected to the U.S. Senate from Tennessee, in 1967, he served until 1985, including two terms as Minority Leader (1977-1981) and two terms as Majority Leader (1981-1985). Following undergraduate studies at the University of the South and Tulane University, he received his law degree from the University of Tennessee.

Speaking of Brandeis

Two of the more recent Brandeis Medal recipients chose to speak about Justice Brandeis himself. Supreme Court Associate Justice Ruth Bader Ginsburg's 2003 presentation was titled *From Benjamin to Brandeis to Breyer: Is There A Jewish Seat?*. Supreme Court Associate Justice Stephen G. Breyer's 2004 lecture was on *Justice Brandeis as Legal Seer*. Both lectures were published with permission in the Supreme Court Historical Society Quarterly newsletter in abridged versions.

The articles are reprinted on the following pages.

From Benjamin to Brandeis to Breyer:
Is There A Jewish Seat?

Justice Ruth Bader Ginsburg

I am pleased to speak to students, faculty, and friends of this Law School, the University, and the Louisville community, to which the great Justice, Louis D. Brandeis, was so deeply attached. Between 1924 and 1929, Brandeis donated substantial segments of his library to the University, along with funds to cover the costs of binding, cataloguing, shelving, and supplementing the collection. He described his aim in a letter to his brother:

> Money alone cannot build a worthy University. . . . To become great, a University must express the people whom it serves, . . . the people and the community at their best. The aim must be high and the vision broad; the goal seemingly attainable but beyond the immediate reach.

To his nephew, who would superintend the Brandeis donation, he wrote of his conception of the role of the donor with captivating simplicity:

> They are to build up a library. You and I are to help them. . . . [I]t is my purpose to continue to help them . . . .

The good Dean, at my request, was kind enough to schedule this lecture before night sets in. May I borrow from Brandeis in explaining the reason for my request. Brandeis counseled the Trustees of the University to meet in the mornings and afternoons. In the evenings, he said, and I might add, especially after a good dinner, "the vitality and energies are spent and . . . judgment [is] naturally impaired." In 1993, the U.S. Supreme Court Historical Society sponsored a five-part lecture series on the Jewish Justices from Brandeis to Fortas. My aim in this lecture is first to describe an earlier figure, the first Jew nominated to serve on the U.S. Supreme Court. Then, after returning to Brandeis, I will endeavor to explain why I believe there will be no supplement to the Historical Society series ranking Justice Stephen Breyer and me as the sixth and seventh Jewish Justices.

The man who might have preceded Justice Brandeis by some sixty-three years as first Jewish member of the Supreme Court had a less secure start in life than Brandeis did, and a less saintly character. His name was Judah P. Benjamin. His career path is intriguing.

Born in 1811 in St. Croix in the Virgin Islands, the son of Sephardic Jews, Benjamin grew up in Charleston, South Carolina, and became a celebrated lawyer in ante-bellum

New Orleans. Though his boyhood, unlike Brandeis', was heavily steeped in Jewish culture, as an adult, he married outside the faith in a Catholic ceremony, and did not keep Jewish laws or celebrate Jewish holidays. Yet he could not escape his Jewish identity. The world in which he lived would not allow him to do that.

In 1853, President Millard Fillmore nominated Benjamin to become an Associate Justice of the United States Supreme Court. Elected the preceding year as one of Louisiana's two U.S. Senators, Benjamin declined the High Court nomination. His preference for the Senate suggests that the Supreme Court had not yet become the co-equal Branch of Government it is today. Benjamin was the first acknowledged Jew to hold a U.S. Senate seat; he was elected, in 1858, to a second six-year term.

Had Benjamin accepted the Supreme Court post, his service likely would have been shorter than the nine and a half years I have already served as a Justice (and far shorter than Brandeis' twenty-three years). In early 1861, in the wake of Louisiana's secession from the Union, Benjamin resigned the Senate seat for which he had forsaken the justiceship. He probably would have resigned a seat on the Court had he held one.

Benjamin is perhaps best known in the United States for his stirring orations in the pre-Civil War Senate on behalf of Southern interests—orations expressing sentiments with which we would today no doubt disagree—and later for his service as Attorney General, Secretary of War, and finally Secretary of State in the Confederate cabinet of Jefferson Davis. Although Benjamin achieved high office, he lived through a time of virulent anti-Semitism

Justice Ginsburg at an open forum with Brandeis law students.

in America. Political enemies called him Judas Iscariot Benjamin. He was ridiculed for his Jewishness in the press, by military leaders on both sides (by Northern General Ulysses S. Grant, and Southern General "Stonewall" Jackson), and even by fellow Confederate politicians.

After the Confederate surrender, Benjamin fled to England; en route, he narrowly survived close encounters with victorious Union troops, rough waters, and storms at sea. Benjamin's political ventures in the U.S. Senate and in the Confederacy of Southern States were bracketed by two discrete but equally remarkable legal careers, the first in New Orleans, the second in Britain.

Having left Yale College after two years without completing the requirements for a degree, and under cloudy circumstances, Benjamin came to New Orleans in 1832 to seek his fortune. He studied and worked hard, and was called to the bar that same year. Although he struggled initially, his fame and wealth grew large after the publication, in 1834, of a Digest of Reported Decisions of the Supreme Court of Louisiana and of that tribunal's pre-Statehood predecessor. Benjamin's book treated comprehensively for the first time Louisiana's uniquely cosmopolitan and complex legal system, derived from Roman, Spanish, French, and English sources. Benjamin's flourishing practice and the public attention he garnered helped to propel his 1852 election by the Louisiana Legislature to the United States Senate. (Recall that until 1913, when the Seventeenth Amendment became effective, U.S. Senators were chosen not directly by the People, but by the Legislatures of the several States.)

Benjamin's fortune plummeted with the defeat of the Confederacy. He arrived in England with little money and most of his property lost or confiscated. His Louisiana Creole wife and a daughter reared Catholic had long before settled in Paris; they anticipated continuing support from Benjamin in the comfortable style to which they had grown accustomed. He nevertheless resisted business opportunities in the French capital, preferring the independence of a law practice, this time as a British barrister.

Benjamin opted for a second career at the bar notwithstanding the requirement that he start over by enrolling as a student at an Inn of Court and serving an apprenticeship. This, Benjamin's contemporaries reported, he undertook cheerfully and with fabulous industry, although he was doubtless relieved when the Inn of Court to which he belonged, Lincoln's Inn, determined to admit him to full membership after six months rather than the usual three years. Benjamin became a British barrister at age fifty-five. His situation at that mature stage of life closely paralleled conditions of his youth. He was a newly-minted lawyer with a struggling practice, but, he wrote to a friend, "as much interested in my profession as when I first commenced as a boy." Repeating his Louisiana progress, Benjamin made his reputation among his new peers by publication. Drawing on the knowledge of civilian systems gained during his practice in Louisiana, Benjamin produced a work in England that came to be known as Benjamin on Sales. First published in 1868, the book was a near-instant legal classic. Its author was much praised, and Benjamin passed the remainder of his days as a top earning, highly esteemed, mainly appellate advocate. He became a Queens Counsel seven years after his admission to the Bar. His voice was heard in appeals to the House of Lords and the Judicial Committee of the Privy Council in no fewer than 136 reported cases between 1872 and 1882.

A biographer of Benjamin tells us that, "[h]owever desperate his case, Benjamin habitually addressed the court as if it were impossible for him to lose." This indomitable cast of mind characterized both Benjamin's courtroom advocacy and his response to fortune's vicissitudes. He rose to the top of the legal profession twice in one lifetime, on two continents, beginning his first ascent as a raw youth and his second as a fugitive minister of a vanquished power. The London Times, in an obituary, described Judah Benjamin as a man with "that elastic resistance to evil fortune which preserved [his] ancestors through a succession of exiles and plunderings."

The first Jew to accept nomination to the U.S. Supreme Court, of course, was Louis D. Brandeis, who grew up here in Louisville. Brandeis graduated from Harvard Law School in 1876 at age twenty, with the highest scholastic average in that law school's history. He maintained close and continuing relationships with his teachers there, and, at age twenty-six, was called back to lecture on the law of evidence. During his days at the bar, Brandeis was sometimes called "the people's attorney," descriptive of his activity in the great social and economic reform movements of his day. He helped create the pro bono tradition in the United States. Spending at least half his working hours on public causes, Brandeis reimbursed his Boston law firm for the time he devoted to nonpaying matters.

Papers lodged here explain something of which I was unaware until preparing these remarks: his support of women's suffrage. As in other situations, he emphasized the obligations as much as the rights of citizenship. In 1913 he wrote simply and to the point: "We cannot relieve her from the duty of taking part in public affairs." This theme of civic responsibility seems to me Brandeis' lietmotif first as a lawyer, and later, as a judge.

Brandeis made large donations of his wealth from practice to good causes and lived frugally at home. A friend recounted that, whenever he went to the Brandeis house for dinner, he ate before and afterward. Brandeis was appointed to the Court by President Wilson in 1916. Like me, he was sixty years old at the time of his appointment. One of his colleagues, James Clark McReynolds, was openly anti-Semitic, as were some detractors at the time of his nomination. When Brandeis spoke in conference, McReynolds would rise and leave the room. No official photograph was taken of the Court in 1924 because McReynolds refused to sit next to Brandeis, where McReynolds, appointed by Wilson two years before Brandeis, belonged on the basis of seniority.

Most people who encountered Brandeis were of a different view. Chief Justice Charles Evans Hughes described him as "master of both microscope and telescope." Commenting on his ability to transform the little case before him into a larger truth, Holmes said he had the art of seeing the general in the particular. President Franklin Delano Roosevelt, among others, called Brandeis not "Judas," but "Isaiah." Admirers, both Jewish and Gentile, turned to the scriptures to find words adequate to describe his contributions to U.S. constitutional thought. He elaborated the canons of judicial restraint more powerfully than any other jurist, cautioning judges to be ever on guard against "erect[ing] our prejudices into legal principles." At the same time, he was an architect—a master builder—of the constitutional right to privacy and of the modern jurisprudence of free speech. He wrote, most famously:

> Those who won our independence believed that the final end of the State was to make men free to develop their faculties; and that in its government the deliberative forces should prevail over the arbitrary. They valued liberty both as an end and as a means. They believed liberty to be the secret of happiness and courage to be the secret of liberty. They believed that freedom to think as you will and to speak as you think are means indispensable to the discovery and spread of political truth; that without free speech and assembly discussion would be futile; that with them, discussion affords ordinarily adequate protection against the dissemination of noxious doctrine; that the greatest menace to freedom is an inert people; that public discussion

is a political duty; and that this should be a fundamental principle of the American government.

Brandeis was not a participant in religious ceremonies or services, but he was an ardent Zionist, and he encouraged the next two Jewish Justices—Cardozo and Frankfurter—to become members of the Zionist Organization of America. Brandeis scholar Melvin Urofsky commented that Brandeis brought three gifts to American Zionism: organizational talent; an ability to set goals and to lead men and women to achieve them; and above all, an idealism that recast Zionist thought in a way that captivated Jews already well-established in the United States. Jews abroad who needed to flee from anti-Semitism, Brandeis urged, would have a home in the land of Israel, a place to build a new society, a fair and open one, he hoped, free from the prejudices that marked much of Europe; Jews comfortably situated in the United States, in a complementary way, would have a mission, an obligation to help their kinsmen build that new land.

When Brandeis retired from the Supreme Court in 1939 at age eighty-three, his colleagues wrote in their farewell letter:

> Your long practical experience and intimate knowledge of affairs, the wide range of your researches and your grasp of the most difficult problems, together with your power of analysis and your thoroughness in exposition, have made your judicial career one of extraordinary distinction and far-reaching influence.

That influence, I can attest, continues to this day.

Law as protector of the oppressed, the poor, the minority, the loner, is evident in the life body of work of Justice Brandeis, as it is in the legacies of Justices Cardozo, Frankfurter, Goldberg, and Fortas, the remaining four of the first five Jewish Justices. Frankfurter, once distressed when the Court rejected his view in a case, reminded his brethren, defensively, that he "belong[ed] to the most vilified and persecuted minority in history." I prefer Arthur Goldberg's affirmative comment: "My concern for justice, for peace, for enlightenment," Goldberg said, "stem[s] from my heritage." The other Jewish Justices could have reached the same judgment. Justice Breyer and I are fortunate to be linked to that heritage.

But Justice Breyer's situation and mine is distinct from that of the first five Jewish Justices. I can best explain the difference by recounting a bit of history called to my attention in remarks made last year by Seth P. Waxman. Seth served with distinction as Solicitor General of the United States from 1997 until January 2001.

Seth spoke of one of his predecessors, Philip Perlman, the first Jewish Solicitor General. Perlman broke with tradition in the 1940s and successfully urged in a friend of the Court brief the unconstitutionality of racially restrictive covenants on real property. The case was *Shelley v. Kraemer*, decided in 1948. The brief for the United States was written by four lawyers, all of them Jewish: Philip Elman, Oscar Davis, Hilbert Zarky, and Stanley Silverberg. All the names, save Perlman's, were deleted from the filed brief. The decision to delete the brief drafters' names was made by Arnold Raum, Perlman's principal assistant and himself a Jew. "It's bad enough," Raum said, "that Perlman's name has to be there." It wouldn't do, he thought, to make it so evident that the position of the United States was "put out by a bunch of Jews."

Consider in that light President Clinton's appointments in 1993 and 1994 of the 107th and 108th Justices, Justice Breyer and me. Our backgrounds had strong resemblances: we had taught law for several years and served on federal courts of appeals for more years. And we are both Jews. In contrast to Frankfurter, Goldberg, and Fortas, however, no one regarded Ginsburg and Breyer as filling a Jewish seat. Both of us take pride in and draw strength from our heritage, but our religion simply was not relevant to President Clinton's appointments.

The security I feel is shown by the command from Deuteronomy displayed in artworks, in Hebrew letters, on three walls and a table in my chambers. "Zedek, Zedek," "Justice, Justice shalt thou pursue," these art works proclaim; they are ever present reminders of what judges must do "that they may thrive." There is also a large silver mezuzah mounted on my door post. It is a gift from the super bright teenage students at the Shulamith School for Girls in Brooklyn, New York, the school one of my dearest law clerks attended.

Jews in the United States, I mean to convey, face few closed doors and do not fear letting the world know who we are. A question stated in various ways is indicative of large advances made. What is the difference between a New York City garment district bookkeeper and a Supreme Court Justice? One generation my life bears witness, the difference between opportunities open to my mother, a bookkeeper, and those open to me.

Not long ago, tapes came to light recording President Nixon's February 1, 1972 conversation with the Reverend Billy Graham, spiritual counselor to several Presidents, including George W. Bush. Graham complained of what he saw as Jewish domination of the news media: "This stranglehold has got to be broken," the Reverend said, "or th[e] country is going down the drain." He added, "[Jews] know I am friendly to Israel, [but] [t]hey don't know how I really feel about what they are doing in this country. . . . They're the ones putting out the pornographic stuff." His parting speculation: "If [Nixon] g[o]t elected a second time, then we might be able to do something [about that]." Thirty years later, Graham expressed dismay and remorse that he could ever have said such things.

True, in recent months, anti-Semitism's ugly head has been visible in our world. Even so, Jews in the United States seldom encounter the harsh anti-Semitism that surrounded Judah Benjamin, or that touched Brandeis, too, when the U.S. Senate debated his nomination. I pray we may keep it that way.

May I now close where I began. Harvard Professor Paul A. Freund, once law clerk to Brandeis, recounted that Brandeis was drawn, first by his mother's encouragement, to the writings of the savant Goethe, and that he particularly liked a passage that translates: "You must labor to possess that which you have inherited." Brandeis endowed this University with his books and papers to make it, in his words, "rich in ideals and eager in the desire to attain them." I wish the University continuing success as it labors to build and maintain the worthy institution Brandeis envisioned.

Justice Brandeis as Legal Seer

Justice Stephen G. Breyer
Associate Justice, United States Supreme Court

I am pleased indeed to be here in Louisville. It is an honor to be asked to give this lecture, associated with Justice Louis Brandeis. To set the scene, let me remind you of several basic biographical facts of Brandeis's life.

Louis Brandeis was born here in Louisville in 1856. A few years earlier, his family had left Prague, fearing a conservative reaction to the failed democratic revolution there. The family prospered as merchants and was able to give Louis a good education—both here in Louisville and in Germany, where he attended high school. Although Louis's family was Jewish, they did not observe Jewish customs or religious practices. Louis maintained that secular life, although he felt the influence of his uncle, Lewis Dembitz, a practicing lawyer and orthodox Jew; indeed, he took Dembitz's last name as his middle name.

Brandeis was a brilliant law student, lawyer, and judge. I should like to read an excerpt (quoted by Tom McCraw) from a letter about him written by a fellow student at Harvard Law: Brandeis, it says,

Justice Breyer delivering the Brandeis lecture.

> graduated last year from Law School and is now taking a third year here—was the leader of his class and one of the most brilliant legal minds they have ever had here—and is but little over twenty-one withal. Hails from Louisville—is not a College graduate, but has spent many years in Europe, . . . Tall, well-made, dark, beardless, and with the brightest eyes I ever saw. Is supposed to know everything and to have it always in mind. The Profs. listen to his opinions

with the greatest deference, and it is generally correct. There are traditions of his omniscience floating through the school. One I heard yesterday— A man last year lost his notebook of Agency lectures. He hunted long and found nothing. His friends said—Go and ask Brandeis—he knows everything—perhaps he will know where your book is—He went and asked. Said Brandeis—"Yes—go into the Auditor's room, and look on the west side of the room, and on the sill of the second window, and you will find your book"—And it was so.[1]

This letter suggests that Brandeis was omniscient, indeed, a seer, a matter to which I shall return.

Brandeis's professional accomplishments lived up to his Law School reputation. For thirty years, with his partner Samuel Warren, he practiced law in Boston, where he turned his raw intelligence, powerful legal imagination, unusual capacity for hard work, and love of advocacy into a highly successful career. That is to say, Brandeis did well financially, but he did not ignore the "public interest" dimension of the profession. Indeed, he argued many of his cases without charge, winning most of them, and earning in the process a reputation as "the people's lawyer."

Brandeis became particularly interested in government regulation, which he saw as a weapon to help the ordinary citizen, worker, or consumer. Let me give you some examples of his work on regulation: Marshalling facts, including the "fact" that the railroads were operating inefficiently, he convinced the Interstate Commerce Commission that it should deny significant increases in railroad rates. Filling his famous "Brandeis brief" with "facts" about the effects of working long hours on women's health, he convinced the Supreme Court to uphold as constitutional an Oregon law limiting the number of hours that women could work.[2] (And that was not an easy legal task three years after the Supreme Court had struck down a similar law limiting bakers' hours in *Lochner v. New York*.[3]) Brandeis worked for stronger antitrust laws, for more extensive regulation of big business, and, in particular for a new regulatory agency, the Federal Trade Commission, which, after Woodrow Wilson's election, he helped to establish.

In 1916 President Wilson appointed Brandeis, then 60, to the United States Supreme Court. After contentious hearings, the Senate confirmed Brandeis. He served on the Court for 23 years. His work has had an impact that has lasted for generations.

The question I want to discuss this evening is: Why? Why has Brandeis's reputation as a great lawyer and judge endured for all these years? Is it because, as his classmate's letter suggests, he was a seer, someone who knew everything? Is it because, as Louis Jaffe once told me, he was the greatest liberal of his day? Is it because of his unflagging support for average working people? Court historian Maeva Marcus writes that Brandeis's opinions reflected his experiences with the problems of industrial democracy, including mediating a garment workers' strike.[4] Another scholar, Tom McCraw, argues that

> [t]he central themes of his [C]ourt career accorded well with the chief interests of his earlier life: a preoccupation with actual social conditions, an

insistence on individual rights and autonomy, and ... a powerful commitment to judicial restraint.[5]

He adds that Brandeis's opinions, embodying these themes, made him "an American hero[,] ... a properly revered symbol of individualism, integrity, self-reliance, and willingness to fight hard for cherished values."[6]

I do not quarrel with these assessments, but, in my view, they do not fully explain the lasting impact of Brandeis's work. Brandeis, after all, could not foretell the future; his law school classmates' belief to the contrary notwithstanding. He was a man of his time. And his opinions reflect the social and economic problems of those times. Why, then, does his work still resonate in a world that faces different economic and social problems? Why do we continue to find accurate Tom McCraw's description of Brandeis as embodying "impartiality, wisdom, and judicial depth?"[7]

With this question in mind, I recently re-read one of Brandeis's most famous opinions, his dissent in the *New State Ice Co. v. Liebmann*[8] case. Those reactions may be of interest to you because they come from a judge who very much admires the opinion, yet who has lived nearly a century later than Brandeis in a world with different economic and social problems. Given the differences in perspective, perhaps they will help us locate where in the opinion its enduring value lies.

The Supreme Court decided *New State Ice Co.* in 1932. Oklahoma had enacted a statute regulating firms that sold ice in the State. Any such firm was required to obtain the State's permission to enter the business, pay a licensing fee, charge regulated rates, and follow Commission-set accounting procedures. The Liebmanns, who wanted to enter the ice business, challenged the statute's constitutionality. They pointed to Supreme Court precedent holding that a State could regulate an industry only if that industry was "impressed with a public interest," a matter determined by history or by a special public need for the industry's goods or services. The Liebmanns argued that providing ice was no longer a special "public interest" industry. They argued that providing ice did not differ significantly from providing meat, vegetables, or other ordinary commodities; that new, electric refrigeration permitted ice to be made by almost anyone; and that State regulation primarily served to shield existing ice providers from competition by new entrants. Ultimately a majority of the Court agreed. The Court found that "the practical tendency" of the law was to "shut out new enterprises, and thus create and foster monopoly in the hands of existing establishments, against, rather than in aid of, the interest of the consuming public." The Court struck the statute down as unconstitutional.

Brandeis disagreed with the majority. His 31-page dissenting opinion contains 57 footnotes, almost every one of which is crammed full of facts. I cannot reproduce the opinion here. But I can give you the flavor of it. Brandeis quotes from Lord Hale's Treatise on the Ports of the Sea, from the Ice and Refrigeration Blue Book for 1927, from the magazine Refrigerating World, and from an old Supreme Court opinion that describes the regulation of chimney sweepers. His text and footnotes explain the nature of public utility regulation. They demonstrate that ice manufacturing had become an important industry by the early 1930s (52,202,160 tons were produced in 1927) with widespread industrial, agricultural, and domestic uses. They make clear that, without ice, perishable commodities, such as food, could not be sold at great distances, particularly in states with warm summers such as Oklahoma (where, according to Brandeis, the average "mean normal temperature" from "May to September is 76.4 degrees.").

The text and footnotes show that electric refrigerators, while part of a growing market, had not yet achieved dominance and many families could not afford them. They discuss plant-based economies of scale, using cost figures to suggest that many localities could only support one plant of efficient size. They describe consumer complaints about poor service, and how the state commission sought to provide better service and lower prices. They refer to economists who argued that the economic problem in the 1930s was not high prices, but so-called "destructive competition," and others who believed "that one of the major contributing causes" of the current depression "has been unbridled competition."

One must ask, however, what conclusion the reader is meant to draw from the display of facts and technical arguments. And here we may find differences in the reactions of Brandeis's contemporary readers and those of today. Did Brandeis intend to show that regulation, by restricting competition, would help rescue America from the Depression? A later report from Paul Freund, Justice Brandeis's law clerk, that Brandeis kept a file labeled "Depression Cures," offers some support for this view. That possibility was not considered peculiar at the time; in fact, it found expression in President Roosevelt's effort to enact the National Industrial Recovery Act, a law that would have created industry cartels, where industry leaders, worker representatives, and government members together would have determined prices, product supply, and working conditions in many major industries.

But if the desirability of some such system is what Brandeis sought to prove in his dissent, he failed in the long term. Few industrial economists today believe that competition-restricting devices could have overcome the Depression. Brandeis himself expressed doubts about New Deal measures like the National Industrial Recovery Act, writing to his daughter in 1934 that such cures "seem[ed] to be going from bad to worse." And Brandeis ultimately joined a unanimous Court that struck down the NIRA as a form of "delegation run riot."

Then, was Brandeis trying to show that "destructive competition" was a serious problem demanding a legislative solution? If so, his view no longer reflects the consensus of modern regulatory economists, who think that "destructive competition" was generally an empty pejorative phrase used by established firms in regulated industries like trucking, maritime shipping, or airlines, to stop the competition that new entrants might provide. That is just what the *New State Ice* majority said, namely that the Oklahoma statute would hurt, not help, consumers, by restricting competition.

Was Brandeis trying to show that the ice business was a natural monopoly that the State must regulate to protect the public? If so, economists today might find his reasoning inadequate. The facts that he relied upon—that only one firm supplied ice in most localities, that prices were uniform, that the value of ice was low compared to shipping costs—might or might not show a natural monopoly depending upon the ability of new competitors to enter a market should that single firm seek to raise its prices.

Was Brandeis trying to help small business? It seems not: the Liebmanns' ice company would have been the very kind of small business, seeking to enter an industry dominated by existing firms, that Brandeis would ordinarily have supported, given his opposition to big business and trusts.

Was Brandeis trying to prove that regulation of industry was itself a good idea, helping to protect the public from the harms that "big business" might cause? If so, he has not entirely succeeded over time. The terms of the economic debate have shifted as the American public has become less sanguine about the ability of government regulation to solve our major economic problems. We have seen regulatory agencies "captured" by those whom they are supposed to regulate. We have found instances where government regulation has proved counter-productive. As a consequence, we no longer argue among ourselves in absolute terms—i.e., no regulation or full-blown "command and control" regulation. Rather, we debate more nuanced questions of where, when, and what kind of regulation is appropriate. Brandeis may have seen regulation as an answer; today we see it as a source of questions.

Was Brandeis trying to show that States must have greater regulatory powers in order to help small business, workers, and consumers? If so, the facts of *New State Ice* offer only a modicum of support for that proposition. And the need to augment State powers for that purpose proved less important with the advent of the New Deal. Under Roosevelt, the federal government, not the States, proved the instrument of policy change. The federal government's regulatory powers continued to expand for decades, as late as the 1970s and under Republican as well as Democratic Presidents. Where Brandeis envisioned the States as saving the day, it ended up being Congress that enacted far-reaching regulatory statutes and then established federal agencies to administer them.

If history fails to validate at least some of Brandeis's economic views, however, that fact does not diminish the life and force that his dissenting opinion retains to this day. According to Westlaw, the *New State Ice* decision has been cited 1,679 times, in recent Supreme Court opinions, in untold numbers of law review articles, and elsewhere. Why? I suspect it is because his fact-based discussion helps to support two important general statements, and it embodies an important constitutional attitude.

The first statement concerns the relation of the Supreme Court and the States. Brandeis's opinion says that "[i]t is one of the happy incidents of the federal system that a single courageous state may, if its citizens choose, serve as a laboratory; and try novel social and economic experiments without risk to the rest of the country."[9]

The second statement concerns the relation of the Supreme Court and legislatures. Brandeis, while acknowledging that the Constitution required the Court to strike down arbitrary legislation, added these words:

> But, in the exercise of this high power, we must be ever on our guard, lest we erect our prejudices into legal principles. If we would guide by the light of reason, we must let our minds be bold.[10]

These two statements do not favor or disfavor any particular set of economic or social beliefs. Rather, they describe a structural relationship, a proper structural relationship, between the courts and the Constitution. This relationship means that legislatures, both federal and state, must have broad power to determine the legal relationships among labor, management, capital, and consumers. And courts, when they review legislative decisions about economic and social matters (where basic individual liberties are not threatened) must respect a legislature's judgments.

Seen as an effort to demonstrate the validity of these propositions, Brandeis's lengthy factual descriptions and technical arguments suddenly spring to life. We see them, not as dated claims from the 1930s about what is the case, but as hypothetical claims about what then plausibly might be so—just as Brandeis said they were. (It might be true, for example, that freight costs were so high that local ice plants were immune from competition—even if we cannot be certain.) The change, from the actual to the possible, makes a difference. The opinion's detailed discussion of ice manufacturing, temperature changes, destructive competition, and classic public utility regulation then serve to demonstrate the following lasting truths:

> First, a truth about the world, namely the likely relevance of factual matters to the solution of an economic problem;
>
> Second, a truth about the judiciary, namely the comparative inability of judges to find remedies for substantive economic problems;
>
> Third, a truth about legislatures, namely their comparative advantage when it comes to investigating the facts, understanding their relevance, and finding solutions;
>
> And fourth, a truth about the Constitution, namely its democratic preference for solutions legislated by those whom the people elect.

By using facts to show what plausibly might be so, Brandeis demonstrated the truth of these propositions. This, in my view, is the key to the opinion's greatness and enduring constitutional value.

To repeat what I see as the connection that the *New State Ice* dissent finds between ice-making machinery and human liberty: I see that connection as embodying what Judge Learned Hand described as the "spirit of liberty," that "spirit that is not too sure of itself." That is a message that, I believe, Brandeis thought courts, like other institutions in a democracy, might take into account.

Indeed, Brandeis understood the Constitution's basic objective as the creation of a certain kind of democratic system of government—a system that protects fundamental human liberty while assuring each citizen the right to participate in well-functioning democratic decision-making institutions. That system foresees, and depends upon, citizens deciding for themselves how to live together in their communities. The job of the Court is to keep legislatures on the constitutional rails, deferring to legislators' judgments whenever fundamental individual liberties are not seriously threatened.

This view of the Constitution has been at issue in recent cases in our Court. In *United States v. Lopez*,[11] decided in 1995, the Court struck down a federal statute called the Gun-Free School Zones Act, which made it a federal crime for anyone knowingly to possess a firearm near a school. The majority found that the statute exceeded Congress' authority to legislate under its Commerce Clause power, because possessing a gun in a local school zone was not economic activity that substantially affected interstate commerce. In the view of the minority, the Constitution required us to judge the matter not directly, but at one remove. "Courts," we said, "must give Congress a degree of leeway in determining the existence of a significant factual connection between the regulated activity and interstate commerce—both because the Constitution delegates the commerce power directly to Congress and because the determination requires an empirical judgment of a kind that a legislature is more likely than a court to make with accuracy."[12] The question was not whether there actually was a substantial connection between gun-related school violence and interstate commerce, but whether Congress could rationally have found such a connection. An Appendix, full of reports and studies, tried to show that Congress could have found that gun-related violence near schools is a commercial, not just a human, problem.

More recently, the Court found that Congress had exceeded its enforcement power under the Fourteenth Amendment to enact Title I of the Americans with Disabilities Act.[13] Title I prohibited States from discriminating against the disabled in employment, and it required States to make some accommodations for disabled employees. The Court held that the legislative record was inadequate, because it did not show that Congress had identified a pattern of irrational state discrimination in employment against the disabled or designed an appropriate way to enforce an anti-discrimination requirement. Again, the dissent, citing the mass of facts that Congress had assembled with the help of a special task force on the need for remedial legislation, argued that Congress might reasonably have found a need for its legislation, and that strict judicial review of the "evidence" before Congress was not appropriate. In both cases, the underlying issue concerned the basic Brandeis question - the structural question of the proper relation between the Court and Congress. I cannot prove that Brandeis was right; nor can I even prove that he would have found himself in dissent. But I can say that his view of the proper Constitutional relation has influenced my own views, three-quarters of a century later.

My reading of the *New State Ice* dissent suggests that Brandeis, perhaps, was not seer in respect to details. Whether Brandeis was right or wrong about ice-making and natural monopoly is a contingent matter, not determined by our Constitution. But whether Brandeis was right about political democracy is a non-contingent matter, permanently inscribed in our Constitution. And here *New State Ice* suggests that Brandeis was a seer. He was right in urging deference to legislative judgments, when economic regulation and ordinary social legislation is at issue. And he was right that we must continue to use facts and consequences to distinguish permissible, or better, from impermissible or worse, interpretations of the Constitution and of law.

Brandeis's dissent shows the need for, and provides, a standard that permits courts to separate the contingent from the permanent. Brandeis remains a seer, not because he could find a lost book in class nor because of his use of factual detail, but because of his prescient sense of the role of judges interpreting a Constitution that, while protecting human liberty, even more importantly, creates a democracy.

1. Thomas K. McCraw, Prophets of Regulation 82-83 (1984).
2. Muller v. Oregon, 208 U.S. 412 (1908).
3. 198 U.S. 45 (1905).
4. Maeva Marcus, Louis D. Brandeis and the Laboratories of Democracy, in Federalism and the Judicial Mind: Essays on American Constitutional Law and Politics 76 (Harry n. Scheiber ed., 1992).
5. McCraw, supra note 1, at 135.
6. Id. at 141-42.
7. Id. at 135.
8. 285 U.S. 262 (1932).
9. Id. at 311.
10. Id.
11. 514 U.S. 549 (1995).
12. Id. at 616-617.
13. Bd. of Trusteess. of the Univ. of Ala. v. Garrett, 531 U.S. 356 (2001).

"*Experience* should teach us to be most on our guard to protect liberty when the government's purposes are beneficent."

—*Olmstead v. United States, 277 U.S. 438 (1928)*

Moderator, Roundtable Discussion with Panelists

Bob Edwards is host of the *Bob Edwards Show* on XM Satellite Radio and previously hosted NPR's *Morning Edition* for almost 25 years. A native of Louisville, he received his B.A. from the University of Louisville and his M.A. in communications from American University. He is the author of two books, most recently *Edward R. Murrow and the Birth of Broadcast Journalism*.

Justice Brandeis and Bob Edwards share not only their Louisville roots, but also a strong commitment to free speech issues.

The Sesquicentennial Program

November 13, 2006

Planning a program of speakers for the Sesquicentennial event was challenging because Justice Brandeis was known for his advocacy for and interest in so many issues—virtually all of which are still current today. In the end, it was decided not to try to cover everything. Three historians and major biographers of Justice Brandeis were invited to speak on topics of greatest interest to them. A law professor known for his work on the First Amendment and the role of Justice Brandeis in addressing this issue was the fourth speaker. The summaries of the presentations of each speaker are on the pages that follow. The program also included a roundtable exchange among all speakers, with Bob Edwards as moderator.

Melvin I. Urofsky is a professor of public policy and law at the Virginia Commonwealth University in Richmond. A graduate of Columbia University, with a doctorate in history also from Columbia, he received his J.D. from the University of Virginia in 1983. He has an exemplary record of publication (including more than fifty books and well over a hundred articles) on a wide range of topics, particularly related to Constitutional Law and the Supreme Court. He is perhaps most well known for his many works on Justice Louis D. Brandeis, including: *A Mind of One Piece: Brandeis and American Reform* (1971); *Louis D. Brandeis and the Progressive Tradition* (1980); *Other People's Money* (editor of a new edition of Brandeis's work, 1995); *Letters of Louis D. Brandeis* (a five volume collection edited with David W. Levy); and *The Family Letters of Louis D. Brandeis* (a 2002 book edited with David W. Levy). He is currently completing a biography of Justice Brandeis.

Urofsky has often written about Justice Brandeis and Zionism. This photograph is part of the Brandeis Papers collection and is believed to be Justice Brandeis with a colleague involved in the Zionist effort.

Louis D. Brandeis as Lawyer and Judge

Melvin I. Urofsky

In his lifetime, Louis D. Brandeis was not only a very successful attorney, but his service on the United States Supreme Court has placed him in the highest ranks of justices. As a lawyer, Brandeis helped to pioneer the modern practice of law, that is, the lawyer as counselor as well as advocate, and he was among the first to organize his office according to specialties (even though he himself always remained a generalist). On the Court, his many accomplishments included articulating a constitutional right to privacy, setting forth the modern rationale for the First Amendment's Speech Clause, and beginning the process known as incorporation, by which the Bill of Rights applies to the states through the Fourteenth Amendment's Due Process Clause.

There is a theme that runs through Brandeis's work as a lawyer, as a reformer, and as a justice, and that theme is education. From the beginning Brandeis believed that the law had to reflect the realities of modern life. One of the great strengths of the common law could be found in the old adage he liked to quote, that out of the facts grows the law. But in the latter part of the nineteenth and early part of the twentieth century, the law had become frozen and formal. Rules, most of which had been designed to protect property rights, had been raised to a near-holy status, with their advocates claiming that to ignore these rules would lead to the downfall of the free enterprise system and the freedoms associated with it.

Brandeis, as a lawyer, a reformer, and a judge believed that the reason lawyers and judges clung to these rules was ignorance, especially a lack of knowledge about the social, political and economic facts of modern life. He declared that while one could assume that judges knew the law, one could not assume that they also knew the facts. In his landmark brief in *Muller v. Oregon* (1908) he set out to educate the justices of the nation's highest court on the effect of long hours on women workers, and why the state of Oregon had chosen to enact legislation to protect those workers. One should not view the *Muller* brief in isolation; it was part and parcel of Brandeis's life-long crusade to educate. In all of his appearances before the courts in defense of protective legislation, he strove to inform the judges about the facts, so that the law could conform to the realities of industrial America.

He carried this role on to the Court as well, especially in his dissents. As he explained to Felix Frankfurter, when he wrote for the majority he had to keep his opinions narrowly focused, to avoid alienating his more conservative colleagues. But in dissent, he spoke for himself and whoever chose to join with him. There he could expound and teach. As he would often tell his clerks after going through several drafts of a dissent, "The opinion is now convincing, but how can we make it more instructive?" While working on his dissents in the speech cases he told his law clerk that "the whole purpose, and the only one, is to educate the country."

This made Brandeis not only a powerful advocate before the Court, but an equally potent one as a member. Education, I shall suggest, was the leitmotif that connects Brandeis the lawyer, the reformer, and the justice.

David W. Levy is the David Ross Boyd Professor in the American History Department at the University of Oklahoma. He received his B.A. from the University of Illinois, his M.A. from the University of Chicago, and his Ph.D. from the University of Wisconsin (1967). A prolific author of books and articles, his work covers a number of issues of American intellectual and constitutional history, including topics ranging from the debate over Vietnam to FDR's fireside chats. He has studied and written about Justice Brandeis extensively, including co-editing *The Letters of Louis D. Brandeis* and *The Family Letters of Louis D. Brandeis* (with Melvin I. Urofsky).

Brandeis as Progressive Reformer

David W. Levy

Between his early career as a successful Boston attorney and his later career as a distinguished Associate Justice of the Supreme Court, Louis D. Brandeis was one of the best known progressive reformers in the United States. From the mid-1890s (at about the time that he turned forty) until his appointment to the High Court (a few months before his sixtieth birthday), Brandeis participated in numerous crusades aimed at improving the social, economic, and political life of the American people.

His reforming career began, appropriately enough, at the local level. He enlisted himself in various Boston reform efforts to cleanse municipal government of corruption, improve the local school system, care for the poor and homeless, and resist attempts to monopolize both the city's public transportation system and the big business of distributing natural gas. Soon Brandeis found himself deeply engaged in reform work at the state and regional level, embarking upon long and bitterly acrimonious campaigns to provide affordable life insurance to the citizens of Massachusetts and to prevent the monopolization of New England's railroad transportation. Brandeis's astute management of these campaigns won him national attention and, perhaps inevitably, drew him onto the national stage as a leading advocate of many progressive reforms. His work included efforts to conserve the country's natural resources, to arbitrate major labor-management disputes, to set railroad rates fairly, to defend progressive state legislation before the Supreme Court, to introduce principles of scientific management to American industry, to help organize political forces behind the progressive campaigns of, first, Robert La Follette and then Woodrow Wilson, to aid in the drafting of critical federal legislation, and, perhaps most famously, to oppose the monopolization of American commerce and industry by gigantic corporations. By the time Wilson nominated him to the Supreme Court, Louis Brandeis was one of a handful of progressive reformers whose name was known across the entire country.

In the last generation, historians of early twentieth-century progressivism have pointed out that it was an extremely diverse and multi-faceted effort, a war that occurred on many fronts. It attracted men and women who came to reform activity with widely differing philosophic, economic, and social assumptions and with widely differing reform concerns. They often disagreed with one another on some central questions: immigration restriction, race relations, prohibition of alcohol, women's suffrage, regulation of the trusts, the role of the federal government, and many others. It is important to ask, therefore, what sort of a progressive was Louis Brandeis? What principles and concerns governed *his* reform work?

Brandeis believed that "bigness" was a curse and that the nation's health and welfare depended on combating it. He applied this animosity to bigness both to industry and to government. He had an unbounded faith in the ability of the American people to govern themselves wisely and democratically. In order to do so, however, they must be free to speak and to listen. He strove for middle ground between socialism and unrestricted free-enterprise capitalism; he believed in labor's right to organize and to press its demands with vigor; he was a great defender of social experimentation at the local and state level. His reform efforts were directed mostly at the economic and political ills of the nation; he played almost no part in those branches of the progressive movement that aimed at race relations, the settlement house movement, prohibition of alcohol, or an end to prostitution. He had a healthy respect for reality and a healthy suspicion of utopian schemes. Therefore, he gave long and laborious study to the statistics of American social and economic life. He had impressive principles, but he also did his homework and was rarely, if ever, tripped up by not knowing some matter of fact.

By the start of President Wilson's first administration, Brandeis was spending more and more time in Washington, D.C. And so universal was the admiration and respect that he commanded among progressive politicians and reformers—even among many of those who were directly opposed to some of his views—that dozens of political officials and social reformers regularly sought him out to solicit his advice and ask for his support. A glance at the letters he wrote home at the close of every long Washington day reveals instantly that Louis Brandeis stood at the heart of the national effort to reform American life. If the progressivism was ever a "movement" at all (and some historians think it never achieved that degree of coherence), it was because of a very small number of widely esteemed individuals whose contacts across the reform spectrum enabled diverse activists to come together at critical moments despite their differences. Louis Brandeis was surely one of these unifying forces in American progressivism. It is not too much to say that if he had never served on the Supreme Court at all, he would still be known to American history as one of the nation's leading social reformers of the early twentieth century.

Philippa Strum, Director of the Division of United States Studies at the Woodrow Wilson International Center for Scholars, is also Broeklundian Professor of Political Science Emerita at City University of New York-Brooklyn College and the Graduate Center. She received her B.A. from Brandeis University, Ed. M. from Harvard, and Ph.D. from the Graduate Faculty of The New School (1964). The author and editor of many books and articles on a wide range of topics, including American government, women and politics, civil liberties and human rights, immigration, and Muslims in the United States, she has written or edited a number of works on Justice Brandeis. These include *Louis D. Brandeis: Justice for the People*; *Brandeis: Beyond Progressivism*; and *Brandeis on Democracy*; as well as "The Innovative Lawyering of Louis D. Brandeis," "Louis D. Brandeis as Lawyer and Judge," "Brandeis and the Constitution," "Louis D. Brandeis, the New Freedom and the State," and "Brandeis and Roosevelt."

Louis Dembitz Brandeis:
The Public Activist and Freedom of Speech

Philippa Strum

One of Louis D. Brandeis' many great accomplishments as a jurist was his articulation of the reasoning that now lies at the heart of this nation's free speech jurisprudence. It is to be found particularly in his opinion in *Whitney v. California* (1927), where he stated that "freedom to think as you will and to speak as you think are means indispensable to the discovery and spread of political truth." In a formulation that sounds radical even to today's ears, Brandeis asserted that "[T]he fact that speech is likely to result in some violence or in destruction of property is not enough to justify its suppression. There must be the probability of serious injury to the State."

It is nonetheless not Brandeis' words but Oliver Wendell Holmes' "clear and present danger" formulation that is the stuff of every civics textbook, in spite of the fact that Holmes' comparatively repressive approach to speech was that of a cynic who believed the government had a right to repress speech it considered dangerous. To Holmes, an insistent social Darwinist, speech didn't much matter, as ideas heard and adopted or rejected by the country would make no difference to the future of the human race. Natural law insured that the "fittest" human beings would survive and shape society in their image, whatever speech was or was not allowed.

Before his own elevation to the Supreme Court, Holmes had been a soldier, a lawyer, and a state judge. He was a relative stranger to the political sphere. Brandeis, however, was not. Sixty years old when he joined the Supreme Court in 1916, he had spent a major part of his adult life participating in public affairs. In 1884, as a young lawyer, Brandeis wrote to his brother that he had begun a "public career," and indeed he had. In the next three decades, he would become an activist in a wide variety of causes—utility rates, savings bank life insurance, conservation, unionism, women suffrage, Zionism—and in all of them, he savored and made impressive use of the right to free speech.

His letters from his pre-Court career are in fact filled with the word "speech": reports of speeches he delivered before state legislatures and commissions, the U.S. Congress, and a host of federal agencies; speeches while he was campaigning for Woodrow Wilson in 1912 and organizing for Zionism beginning in 1914; speeches to unions, businessmen's clubs, good government associations, schools, and religious groups. When Brandeis was immersed in a campaign on behalf of the public, he spoke and wrote ceaselessly. He urged his allies to do so as well. "Have editorials and similar notices in various papers, particularly the Springfield Republican, the Worcester Spy, and the Pittsfield papers," he enjoined his troops. "Have personal letters written to members from the Metropolitan District, particularly from Boston, by their constituents…We rely upon you for hard work."

He believed that speech, or communication, was the lifeblood of democracy, and that democracy held the promise of human advancement. Convinced that reasonable people

81

would ultimately come to accept the truth as he saw it, he was unfazed when faced with well-meaning dissent. "Differences in opinions are not only natural but desirable where the question is difficult; for only through such differences do we secure that light and fuller understanding which are necessary to a wise decision," he declared—a lesson gained from his public activism and from his knowledge that his own ideas had changed as that activism brought him into contact with people of many opinions.

It was his life as much as his philosophy, then, that primed him to give speech the greatest possible latitude when he joined the Court. And, in the opinions he wrote between 1920 and 1927, that is precisely what he did, thereby becoming the father of the uniquely permissive approach to speech that this country enjoys today.

"*Fear of serious injury* cannot alone justify suppression of free speech and assembly. Men feared witches and burnt women. It is the function of speech to free men from the bondage of irrational fears. To justify suppression of free speech there must be reasonable ground to fear that serious evil will result if free speech is practiced. There must be reasonable ground to believe that the danger apprehended is imminent. There must be reasonable ground to belief that the evil to be prevented is a serious one."

—*Whitney v. People of State of California*, 274 U.S. 357 (1927).

Erwin Chemerinsky is the Alston & Bird Professor of Law and Professor of Political Science at Duke University. He received his B.S. from Northwestern University and his J.D. from Harvard Law School (1978). He has written extensively on topics of federal jurisdiction and constitutional law, and is a frequent contributor to newspapers and magazines and a commentator on legal issues for the national media. He has argued a number of First Amendment cases before appellate courts and the Supreme Court. He was named in 2005 by Legal Affairs as one of the "top 20 legal thinkers in America."

Rediscovering Brandeis' Right to Privacy

Erwin Chemerinsky

Many years before he became a Supreme Court Justice, Louis Brandeis co-authored one of the most renowned law review articles in American history. Warren and Brandeis, *The Right to Privacy*, 4 Harvard Law Review 193 (1890). Although there was scarcely a mention of "privacy" in the first century of Supreme Court decisions, in the last half century, the Supreme Court expressly invoked privacy in many controversial constitutional cases. For example, the Court used the right to privacy to protect the right to purchase and use contraceptives, the right to abortion, and the right to engage in private, consensual homosexual activity.

Interestingly, the Warren and Brandeis article did not consider privacy in this sense at all. Warren and Brandeis were primarily concerned about how private information about individuals was being publicly disseminated. Their focus was on informational privacy, not autonomy for important personal decisions.

However, the Supreme Court in protecting privacy has rarely considered informational privacy. To this point, there is little constitutional protection against the government revealing and disseminating even highly private information about individuals.

Ironically, the heated debate over whether the Constitution protects privacy in areas such as contraception, abortion, and sexual activity makes it less likely that the Court will develop other privacy rights, such as in the area of informational privacy. This is unfortunate because technological

Justice Brandeis is particularly known for his concern for the right to privacy—the right to be left alone. He and his colleague, Samuel Warren, wrote "The Right to Privacy," published in Harvard Law Review, in which his philosophy on privacy was presented.

developments make protection of informational privacy imperative in the years ahead.

My focus develops three major points. First, the use of a single label, privacy, for divergent concepts has had undesirable consequences. Constitutional protection for privacy includes safeguards from unwarranted government intrusion such as through the Fourth Amendment; guarantees of autonomy such as in the contraception and abortion cases; and protections for information individuals wish to keep secret. The law in each, at times, is confused or inadequately developed because of a lack of clarity as to the different rights involved.

Second, of all of these conceptions of privacy, the least developed constitutionally is informational privacy, the focus of Warren and Brandeis. For example, no Supreme Court case ever has found constitutional protection from public disclosure of private facts and courts of appeals have expressly rejected the existence of such a right.

Third, development of a right to informational privacy is desirable and even essential in the years ahead. Technology, from the human genome project to the internet, demand development of constitutional protections for informational privacy.

Bibliography

Prepared by Peter Scott Campbell

Writings by Brandeis

"The Right to Privacy," 4 Harvard Law Review 193 (1890). With Samuel D. Warren.

Other People's Money, and How the Bankers Use It. New York: Frederick A. Stokes Company, 1914.

The Social and Economic Views of Mr. Justice Brandeis. Edited by Alfred Lief. New York: The Vanguard Press, 1930.

Business—A Profession. Boston: Hale, Cushman & Flint, 1933.

The Curse of Bigness. Edited by Osmond K. Fraenkel. New York: The Viking Press, 1934.

The Brandeis Guide to the Modern World. Edited by Alfred Lief. Boston: Little, Brown and Company, 1941.

Brandeis on Zionism. Edited by Solomon Goldman. Washington, D.C.: The Zionist Organization of America, 1942.

The Words of Justice Brandeis. Edited by Solomon Goldman. New York: Henry Schumann, 1953.

The Unpublished Opinions of Mr. Justice Brandeis; The Supreme Court at Work. Edited by Alexander M. Bickel. Cambridge, Mississippi, 1957.

The Letters of Louis D. Brandeis. 5 volumes. Edited by Melvin I. Urofsky and David W. Levy. Albany: State University of New York Press, 1971-1978.

Brandeis on Democracy. Edited by Philippa Strum. Lawrence: University Press of Kansas, 1995.

The Family Letters of Louis D. Brandeis. Edited by Melvin I. Urofsky and David W. Levy. Norman: University of Oklahoma, 2002.

Biographies and Other Writings About Brandeis

Alfred Lief, *Brandeis; The Personal History of an American Ideal*. New York: Stackpole Sons, 1936.

Alpheus Thomas Mason, *The Brandeis Way: A Case Study in the Workings of Democracy*. Princeton, New Jersey: Princeton University Press, 1938.

Alpheus Thomas Mason, *Brandeis, A Free Man's Life*. New York: The Viking Press, 1946.

Melvin I. Urofsky, *A Mind of One Piece: Brandeis and American Reform*. New York: Charles Scribner's Sons, 1971.

Allon Gal, *Brandeis of Boston*. Cambridge, Massachusetts: Harvard University Press, 1980.

Nelson L. Dawson, *Louis D. Brandeis, Felix Frankfurter, and the New Deal*. Hamden, Connecticut: Archon Books, 1980.

Lewis J. Paper, *Brandeis*. Englewood Cliffs, N.J.: Prentice-Hall, Inc., 1983.

Leonard Baker, *Brandeis and Frankfurter: A Dual Biography*. New York: Harper & Row, 1984.

Philippa Strum, *Louis D. Brandeis: Justice For The People*. Cambridge, Massachusetts: Harvard University Press, 1984.

Brandeis and America. Edited by Nelson L. Dawson. Lexington: University of Kentucky Press, 1989.

Philippa Strum, *Brandeis: Beyond Progressivism*. Lawrence: University Press of Kansas, 1993.

Stephen W. Baskerville, *Of Laws and Limitations: An Intellectual Portrait of Louis Dembitz Brandeis*. Cranbury, New Jersey: Associated University Presses, 1994.